Advance Praise for
"Your Mid-Career GPS"

"This book is for those of you who feel like you know everything and nothing about what's next, you can't fathom writing yet another cover letter, and you wonder "why bother" when it comes to updating your résumé. *If you are feeling alone on this journey, bring this book, and all of the insight and tools it contains, along with you. You will have John's company along the path and you will be one step closer to finding your way!"*

Natalie Siston
Best-selling author of Let Her Out:
Reclaim Who You Have Always Been
Founder, Small Town Leadership

"John lays out a perfect roadmap to help you find your way to career satisfaction! Whether you're not sure if you should stay straight on the road you're on or look for the next turn onto a different path, he will give you simple techniques to understand what you truly want and how to make

it happen. You will begin to fall in love with your journey!"

Jennifer Miller
Project Director | Health Coach

"John expertly guides readers through the trials, tribulations, and common pitfalls of mid-career professionals and managers. He also provides information on the effective career strategies and mindset needed to be successful. This book is a must read if you are looking for professional support and could use a career GPS!"

Porschia Parker Griffin
Founder and CEO of Fly-High Coaching Millennial Coaching Institute

"LinkedIn is the most powerful tool to help you network, build professional relationships, learn, search for jobs, and much more. I always say if you are not on LinkedIn you might be left out. Your Mid-Career GPS provides valuable tips and guidance to help you navigate LinkedIn and start growing your network and create your next advancement opportunity."

Rhonda L. Sher
LinkedIn Specialist, Author, Speaker

"When driving somewhere unfamiliar, I rely on navigation apps for guidance. This book provides that type of assistance for stepping into the unknown with your career. John shares his personal anecdotes throughout and brings to life the tools and techniques he is introducing. How I made it through several detours in my career without this kind of guidance, I will never know. Wherever you are in your career, John has helpful tools and ideas to support your plan!"

Dean Cox
Leadership and Team Effectiveness Coach
Strongest Link Coaching and Consulting, LLC

"John brings to his readers a great combination of personal and professional insight to the awkward journey of navigating career change. John takes what is often found to be daunting and overwhelming into a Mid-Career GPS outlined journey that is manageable for all."

Brian Hedlund
Strategic Partner | PrideStaff

"Maybe you're feeling stuck in your career. Maybe you actually love your job and career but there's

*still that nagging feeling in the back of your head telling you there is something more out there, or maybe you're somewhere in between. Regardless of where you are in your career, the strategies outlined in **Your Mid-Career GPS: Four Steps to Figuring Our What's Next** provides you with thought-provoking questions to help you navigate, but most importantly, tangible actions to take that will help land you in your right next step."*

Jessi Shuraleff
Podcast Host – This Is My Truth

"Because of the pandemic, more and more companies have shifted to using virtual platforms for meetings and interviews. How you SHOW UP virtually is important to making that professional connection. John provides relevant, easy, and useful tips to help you navigate this virtual space."

Robert Rinkewich
Founder and Owner, Vision Photo and Video, LLC

"I am not impressed easily... but John Neral impresses me. If you are serious about your evolution as a professional, then allow him to impress upon you his wisdom and guidance. Not only in this well-thought-out book but also with

him as a coach. John genuinely cares, is real, is tough, and will get you results. His growth and expertise in this space over the past many years has been mind-blowing. Read the book, listen to John, and your future will never be the same!"

Jeffrey St. Laurent
Author, Entrepreneur, Athlete, Dad

"I entrusted the start of my entrepreneurial journey to John because of his unique and qualified experiences that gave me great guidance. This book is a must-read because it captures his invaluable wisdom that will benefit every reader. It's so comforting to have clear and accurate directions as you embark on your professional journey!!!"

D'Ivonne Holman
Fundraising Consultant

"For anyone going through a career slump or looking for something new, this book is definitely for you. John Neral's latest book is a guide for someone like you. It gives simplistic methods to help anyone who has recently lost their job in the pandemic or simply looking to refresh their résumé

and skills. John highlights key areas that many neglect when even using social media to better highlight their skills and abilities. He also uses acronyms and personal reflections to grasp the reader and encourage them in the sometimes daunting process when advancing one's career. If you are that person needing a change or just a refresher for job hunting, then this book is for you!"

Alethea Felton
Holistic Health Coach

"John uses his experience and expertise to guide you in business, but what matters to me is the fact that he has an incredible heart for service and a desire to help others succeed in life. His passion is evident in his coaching, his podcast, and his writings. I have had the opportunity to be one of John's mentors in bowling, but I was always inspired by his passion for connecting and leading those around him, which has in many ways made him a mentor to me."

Heather Bassham Sumlin
Director of Performance Programs
Master Level Instructor
Mental Management Systems

Your Mid-Career GPS –

Four Steps to Figuring Out What's Next

John Neral

Copyright © 2021 by John Neral Coaching, LLC
All rights reserved.

Published and Distributed in Canada by LLH Publishing Inc. **www.andreaseydel.com**[1]
All rights reserved. No part of this book may be reproduced by any mechanical,
photographic, or electronic process, or in the form of a phonograph recording: Nor may it be
stored in a retrieval system, transmitted, or otherwise be copied for public or private use-
other than for "fair use" as brief quotations embodied in articles and reviews without prior
written permission of the publisher. If you use any of the information in this book for
yourself, which is your constitutional right, the author and the publisher assume no
responsibility for your actions.
Library of Congress Cataloging-in-Publication Data
Neral, John
Your Mid-Career GPS - Four Steps to Figuring Out What's Next
\ John Neral
1. Nonfiction > Business & Economics > Careers > Job Hunting
2. Nonfiction > Business & Economics > Mentoring & Coaching
978-1-990461-01-9
LLH Publishing House

1st Printing: July 2021. Printed in USA
Cover Photo Credit: Bruno Bergher
Editor: Richard Lucey, Jr.

Publisher's Note & Author DISCLAIMER
This publication is designed to provide accurate and authoritative information concerning the
subject matter covered. It is sold to understand that the publisher and author are not
engaging in or rendering any psychological, medical or other professional services. If expert
assistance or counselling is needed, seek the services of a competent medical professional.
For immediate support, call your local crisis line. Be Well.

Dedication

To Richard,
For being my greatest cheerleader and advocate
on our incredible personal and professional
journey

To My Dearest and Closest Friends,
For supporting me on this fantastic adventure

To the Job Seekers,
For never giving up on your dreams
because you are more than enough

To the Leaders,
For SHOWing UP each day at your best
so you can make the impact you want

Contents

Foreword

_____

You'll get mixed up, of course,
as you already know.
You'll get mixed up
with many strange birds as you go.
So be sure when you step.
Step with great care and great tact
and remember that Life's
a Great Balancing Act.
Just never forget to be dexterous and deft.
And never mix up your right foot with your left.

And will you succeed?
Yes! You will, indeed!

(98 and 3/4 percent guaranteed.)

KID, YOU'LL MOVE MOUNTAINS!

from *Oh, the Places You'll Go!* by Dr. Seuss

As you begin, or continue, your mid-career journey, I can't help but think of the words of Dr. Seuss. *Oh, the Places You'll Go!* is commonly gifted at graduation, but I believe it can also serve you as you face any "next step" in your life and career. That's what you are about to do as you venture on this journey with my colleague and dear friend John Neral. Here's a bit on how he has shaped my journey so you can see how he will help you on the following pages.

It was the winter of 2018 and I was in Texas sitting in the most tricked-out Starbucks I have ever seen. I was with John and our dear friend Tracy. We were each talking about our "next chapter." Mine was full of ideas and action and excitement and fear and doubt. And John looked at me and said, "You aren't building a business, you are building a movement." At that moment, I don't think I knew that John was helping me create my Mid-Career GPS (he likely didn't either). From that powerful coaching statement blossomed my mid-career pivot, one that has taken me into a corporate dream job, start-up experiences, and a self-employed journey.

I founded Small Town Leadership while working a director-level job at a Fortune 100 Company. In the wee hours of the mornings and nights, I would work on my "passion project." Eventually, that passion project led to a full itinerary of speaking engagements, coaching portfolio, and thousands of words written across blogs and social media platforms. I was so busy that I had to use vacation days to do more work.

I was planning to leave my corporate job to pursue my passion full time, but a dream job became available at the company. The job description included things like: Speak and write about coaching to large audiences. Help company leaders develop coaching skills. Modernize curriculum for adult learners. Motivate a team of professional coaches. I was in. My passion project was paying off in my "day job" in an unexpected and exciting way.

I loved the job, but the work I continued to do outside of my role was pulling me in a different direction and the time came for me to take the most important exit on my mid-career journey. It happened to collide directly with the Covid-19 pandemic. I thought about holding off on taking the leap, but one night, I had an "aha" moment. I asked myself "Who quits her job in the middle of a global pandemic?" Then the answer hit me: "Someone whose dreams are bigger than her fears."

I got off on that exit and there was no turning back.

At every pivot on this path, John was my first call on speed dial. My favorite time to make a call was from the company parking garage before I began my commute home. (This is one of the only things I miss about commuting). John helped me see around corners, prepare for blind spots, and even encouraged me to put the pedal to the metal on several occasions so I could get to my destination sooner.

We talked about the inevitable "bad boss" moments. We chatted about getting psyched up and mentally prepared for interviews and networking meetings. We talked about failure, setback, and disappointment. Most of all, we talked about what was possible when you set a goal and put in the necessary work to move toward it, and eventually reach the destination.

That's exactly what John will talk to you about on the following pages. I know he wants each of you to also be able to call him on speed dial, but this is his way to be of service to you as you continue your career journey.

Mid-career, especially mid-career mid- and post-pandemic, is tough. You feel like you know everything and nothing about what's next. You can't fathom writing yet another cover letter. You wonder "why bother" when it comes to updating your résumé. And you might even feel completely alone - like you are stranded in the middle of an open road - as you ponder which way to turn next.

Consider *Your Mid-Career GPS* the water in the oasis that will help you continue on your path in a purposeful and powerful way. Dig in. Do the work. SHOW UP. Your life, and those you love and serve, will be better for it.

Natalie Siston
Bestselling author of *Let Her Out: Reclaim Who You Have Always Been*
Founder, Small Town Leadership

Introduction

My career path has been messy. It's had its share of ups, downs, spirals, and turns. There were incredible moments of joy, along with sheer frustration, pain, and stress. I've worked with some of the most memorable and incredibly talented people you could imagine. I've also worked with a few people who weren't my favorites, but I have learned a ton from them and will always be grateful. And I've learned this is very common.

In Herminia Ibarra's Harvard Business Review article, "Reinventing Your Career in the Time of Coronavirus," Ibarra states, "Even in happier times, career change is never a perfectly linear process. It's a necessarily messy journey of exploration – and to do it right, you have to experiment with, test, and learn about a range of possible selves."

Reinventing your career isn't new. We've been doing this as long as there has been "work." But the pandemic made us pause, reflect, and consider what's next for us professionally, perhaps a little more than during pre-pandemic times. That's why you need a plan to help you get wherever you are going professionally, and it's why I believe having a GPS is vital to your success.

Your career path is defined by particular moments where you've fought for whatever you wanted – be it a promotion, more responsibility, increase compensation, or more time with family. It's during these moments when you are entirely committed and engaged in achieving the goals you've promised yourself and you are not going to settle. And while the outcome is important, you can't overlook the steps you took to get there. Yet, sometimes, when people hit mid-career, they forget what those steps were.

You're reading this book because you are feeling stuck in your career or feeling undervalued. You know you are capable of more. It has been years since you graduated high school or college, and you are easily overwhelmed by all of the things you think you need to do. And while you know you should get your résumé updated, the problem is you can't find it, or it's been years since you've written one. You believe you should be more engaged on LinkedIn but don't know how to do that. You say you aren't good at networking and interviewing, yet you know these things are integral to your success. Your thinking is continually putting you in a deficit, rather than focusing on what you are good at and taking a realistic inventory of where you can improve. You lie awake at night worrying about how you will navigate this career transition, and at times, it's too much. It's one of the many things keeping you up at night.

If you attended college, I'm willing to bet there was a time when everything flowed. You moved through the process. You enrolled, got accepted, took your courses, and four years later, exited with a degree, and hopefully, a job. You thought you had it all figured out. You knew what to do and were getting acclimated to that thing we call "adulting."

Now, you may feel far removed from that time. Your strategic career plans may have derailed a bit, leaving you feeling alone, perhaps a bit shameful, and beating yourself up because you believe you should have figured this all out by now. You fear being perceived as irresponsible for not liking your job or wanting a change, but you don't want to settle. You haven't come this far to settle. You refuse to let go of your dreams.

What if you made a decision that you were going to welcome all of the new opportunities coming your way? Reading this book is one of the first things you will do to helping you build Your Mid-Career GPS, and it's a great place to start.

It can be challenging to make a change mid-career. I know because I did it on several occasions. Many people doubted or questioned my career moves and gave me a reason to think I was foolish. It's time to quiet the noise and get clear about what *you* want. Making a career change is just a circumstance. Your thoughts around an upcoming career change are an opportunity for you to hear what's going on inside your head and decide how to help you take action.

This change for you is personal and may look very different from other mid-career professionals' changes. For example, you may be seeking an internal promotion because you have spent several years at a company, have done great work, and value loyalty, so you want to stay and see if there is still room for you to grow.

You may have all the information you need to know that there isn't a path upward for you at your current organization. Thus, you are looking to leverage your talents and expertise, take them to a new organization, seek a new and perhaps, more exciting title, and increase your salary. You want to work somewhere you feel more valued.

You may be looking to do something completely different. Navigating a career pivot can undoubtedly be exciting, but may cause tons of questions about whether or not such an opportunity is possible.

People struggle with SHOWing UP when they are fearful of the outcome. We are accustomed to ruminating on potential outcomes, only to waste energy about how things will play out, ultimately holding ourselves back from going after what we want. People often ask me how they can get out of their way. The answer is all about how you want to SHOW UP.

Throughout this book, you will notice that I always write SHOW UP in capital letters. My first book, "SHOW UP – Six Strategies to Lead a More Energetic and Impactful Career," uses SHOW UP as an acronym for these strategies: Set Ground Rules, Have Intentional Conversations, Own Where You Are, Welcome New Opportunities, Use Your Genius, and Protect and Promote Your Brand. As you read this book and see this reference, I hope you will think of SHOWing UP in the context of these six specific strategies, what they mean for you and your career, and reflect your mindset and actions toward SHOWing UP. There is a section devoted to SHOWing UP later in the book.

For this book, I will use the U.S. Office of Personnel Management's (OPM) definition that a mid-career professional is someone with more than 10 years of professional experience. You will reach certain guideposts or mile markers that distinguish the early, middle, and later stages of your career. You have experience. You have achieved some level of success in your work, you've been recognized, and perhaps earned a promotion or two. You are more focused and confident about the work you do and don't want to do. Identifying as a mid-career professional is also a reflection of your mindset.

In my mind, you are a mid-career professional when you identify as being in the "middle" part of your career. I agree with OPM's definition but I also see where some people like to divide their careers into thirds. After graduation, be it high school or college, you could easily have 39-45 years of gainful employment. That means you would define each third based on every 13-15 years. Typically, the majority of my clients fall in that 32-50 age range.

Whether or not you identify as a mid-career professional, the strategies outlined in this book will help you create your career GPS so you can take steps to help you reach whatever professional destination is next for you.

Mid-career professionals may find themselves in a constant battle between maintaining the status quo and doing something they've always dreamed of doing. While they are proud of their accomplishments, there is also a part of them that regrets not obtaining the level of success or recognition they thought they would've achieved by now. Maybe they've lost sight of how amazing they truly are. If this sounds like you, keep reading.

Additionally, by the time mid-career has happened, you've experienced a lot of life events. You may be married or divorced. You may have been in several long-term relationships or trying to figure out what a relationship looks like for you. You have certain hobbies but often struggle with finding time to do them because of your job and family pressures. You may have aging parents and struggle with the difficult shift of being their primary caregiver. I know only too well how difficult and emotionally wrenching that can be. Yet, you get up every morning, put on a happy face, and do the best work you can because that is the kind of person you are.

The clients I work with are heart-centered professionals and leaders. Their default is always to put everyone first, sacrificing their needs for the sake of a project or a dear colleague who needs their help. They struggle to find what work-life balance looks like for them. They know they want it, but they are not sure how to obtain it. Additionally, you find yourself in an energetic battle to keep your tank full. Because you are always giving to others and your employer, you run the risk of burning out at a moment's notice, as your tank seems to always be on or close to empty.

In this book, I will ask you to define certain moments of your career. One of the most defining moments in my career happened in my 11th year as a middle school mathematics teacher. I loved where I was working, the people I was working with, and I certainly had a fantastic time with the students I got to teach every year. One day, as I was beginning to teach a lesson on multiplying fractions, I looked at 25 students' faces staring back at me, and the voice in my head said, "You can't do this anymore." It was as if that voice came out of nowhere, but it was loud, and I needed to listen to it. I felt happy. I enjoyed what I was doing. But I wasn't satisfied knowing that this could be it for the rest of my career. I wasn't ready to settle. As I continued to deliver the lesson, I gave myself permission to question what I was doing with my career and why I wanted more from it. Have you ever had one of those moments?

What transpired over the next few months was an opportunity to honestly evaluate where my career was going and what I wanted. I had a fantastic consulting relationship with a Fortune 500 company along with a successful tutoring business outside of my teaching duties. I was learning that I wanted to shift my focus from teaching students to working with teachers. This would look like some kind of administrative position or an opportunity to level up, but I was unsure of what that was.

I talked to my closest friends and colleagues and told them I was considering making a significant career change. I had my résumé professionally written. I updated my LinkedIn profile. I started networking, looking for jobs, and sharpening my interviewing skills. And then the rejections came.

I got to several last-round interviews for a handful of positions that I not only wanted but also believed I would've been great at, only to learn I wasn't the selected candidate. If someone were kind enough to give me some honest feedback, I would hear things like, "You made it a difficult decision for us, but we went with someone who had more experience." These are comforting words amid disappointment and perhaps something you also have experienced recently.

My opportunity to make such a change came three years later, when I was 40. I accepted a position as a Professional Development Specialist for the District of Columbia Public Schools. In this role, I would work with and supervise 21 instructional coaches across 13 middle schools. I was going to help teachers be better teachers. I got the job I wanted and a fantastic opportunity to stretch and grow. While the job came with an advanced title, it also came with a pay cut. I relocated from New Jersey to Washington, D.C., for a professional and personal opportunity. My husband and I had been dating long distance for two years, and because he was happy with his job, I decided I would be the one to make a move since I was looking for a new job. Yes, you could say I made a move for love, but it was not only for the love of my husband but also for the love of my career. Relocating wasn't part of my plan, but it was a welcomed detour and new destination for my Mid-Career GPS.

That move over 10 years ago accelerated my career. It gave me opportunities I would have never had if I decided to stay in my previous position. I had an opportunity to work as an administrator in a larger and high-profile district. From there, I went to go work at the State Superintendent's Office. From that position, I leveled up to take a job at an educational nonprofit as a Training and Staffing Director. And then, I took an even bigger leap into entrepreneurship. I have never regretted any of these moves, and I continue to have an exciting career. I get to go to work every day. I get to coach amazing clients and help them figure out what's next for them professionally by helping them create their mid-career roadmap to find a job they love or love the job they have. I've launched two podcasts. The first is called #SHOWUP2020 and highlighted everyday people who do extraordinary things because of how they choose to SHOW UP. My second podcast is "The Mid-Career GPS Podcast," and it's an extension of this book. You can listen to it wherever you listen to your favorite podcasts.

I would be remiss if I didn't take some time to talk about a defining and universal moment in all of our careers. That is the effects that the COVID-19 pandemic had on us both personally and professionally. Together, we saw a record number of people unemployed due to the pandemic. According to the Pew Research Center in an article titled, "Unemployment rose higher in three months of COVID-19 than it did in two years of the Great Recession," Rakesh Kochhar writes, "The COVID-19 outbreak and the economic downturn it engendered swelled the ranks of unemployed Americans by more than 14 million, from 6.2 million in February to 20.5 million in May 2020. As a result, the U.S. unemployment rate shot up from 3.8% in February – among the lowest on record in the post-World War II era – to 13.0% in May. That rate was the era's second-highest, trailing only the level reached in April (14.4%)."

We saw industries brought to their knees because life as we knew it had changed. People stopped traveling and staying in hotels. People stopped going to restaurants and instead learned how to cook. While food delivery services saw an uptick, we must acknowledge that many small businesses and restaurants closed because of the pandemic.

Millions of people were either furloughed or laid off. When 2020 began, many companies were positioned to have their best year. Their strategic plans, dreams, and goals quickly changed by late spring when COVID-19 didn't appear to be going away anytime soon.

And with increased vaccinations and a potential return to "normal" on the horizon, it will take years, if not decades, for us to recover from the personal, professional, financial, and mental health impact this pandemic has had.

As an executive and career transition coach, I share this with you because I spent the majority of 2020 working with my clients about what their career roadmap would look like. Just like you, things changed for them. And while 2020 certainly gave us time to reflect and consider, it also hit our savings accounts and checkbooks; affected our mental health, families, and relationships; and caused moments of intense isolation. We missed milestone events and celebrations. Where possible, the majority of the workforce transitioned to a virtual platform, and running out to get your coffee in the morning or midday wasn't something you were typically doing anymore. Gone were the casual, in-person conversations you had with dear friends and colleagues. Gone were the moments when you would stop by someone's office and see if they could take a walk or grab a cup of coffee with you. Now, your dining room table or favorite chair has been turned into your home office or classroom.

2020, in my opinion, will go down as one of the most challenging years for us professionally. Whether you had a job for the entire year or didn't, it took a toll on you. While you were grateful to have a job and a steady paycheck, I know many people who experienced a form of survival guilt and were hesitant to complain about something at work because they had a job and people they knew did not. You may still be unemployed as a result of the pandemic, and I hope the information in this book not only provides you with relevant and tactical strategies to help you navigate and create your mid-career roadmap, but also gives you some inspiration and motivation. Let me ask you this: How would you SHOW UP if you knew your value was non-negotiable? As you go through this book, I hope you will find an answer to that question.

How would you SHOW UP
if you knew your value was non-negotiable?

My book will help you create Your Mid-Career GPS to create a plan to get you from where you are to wherever "Point B" is for you. In this book, I'm leveraging my coach training and experience to help you explore and consider all of the options you have in front of you by asking questions to help you reflect and decide on a course of action you see as best for you. By the end of this book, you are going to have a plan, a roadmap, a GPS to help you chart a path to whatever is next for you professionally. You have an opportunity to go after what you want – this isn't an opportunity for you to settle. Lastly, I have no judgment on any client's decision regarding their career path because I know they are making the best decision for them. This means that I have no personal stake or agenda in how a client reaches their best conclusion. My role is to facilitate the process of helping them get there. Let this book be a guide or a resource to help you create Your Mid-Career GPS.

Throughout this book, you will see a combination of information, both from my experience and experts in various fields, along with coaching questions designed to help you think, reflect, and explore the actions you want to take. They all combine to help you create a step-by-step roadmap, or a personal career GPS, to navigate whatever is next for your career. The ultimate goal is for you to increase your overall job satisfaction, know your value and worth, and be happier than you have ever been professionally.

Periodically, I will share my background and experiences that have helped shape these tips and strategies while supporting that information with research and additional expert information. Some topics in this book are virtually impossible to capture all of the information you may need or question. That is where Google is best. Do not hesitate to put the book down and search for things on Google that have piqued your interest or are not answered in this book.

This book will walk you through four specific stages to help you build Your Mid-Career GPS. In the Prepare section, you will explore your current career situation, along with your attitudes, strengths, and value to help you identify any move you want to make. In the Position section, you will look at best practices for writing your résumé, optimizing your LinkedIn profile, and creating your "Unique Professional Value Statement." Once you have prepared and positioned, the next step is to promote who you are and what you do. In the Promote section, we will talk about building your networking and interviewing skills. More importantly, you will learn how to tell your story from a place of value and service, so you can get people interested in who you are and what you do, rather than just finding you interesting. The last section is an updated version of my #SHOWUP6Strategies. It was important for me to revisit these strategies because of what we experienced in 2020. I've updated these strategies through a lens of helping mid-career professionals SHOW UP to find the best ways they can make an impact and increase their job satisfaction.

Roadmaps are not created overnight. As you navigate the information in this book, you may find yourself taking detours and visiting various topics of interest to you right now. For example, if you pick up this book and have an interview tomorrow, I strongly suggest you immediately jump to the interview section and read it. However, I hope you will move sequentially through these sections. It will help you gain greater insight into the kind of work I do with my clients in helping them create their Mid-Career GPS over several months of working together.

As I say on my podcast, it's time to start building Your Mid-Career GPS. Let's get started!

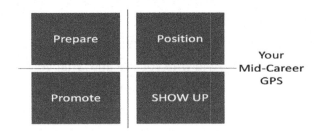

Chapter 1

Prepare – Let's Get Ready for Your Journey

———————

When you prepare for a long trip, you don't just hop in the car and go. You plan. You prepare. You figure out what you need to help you get there with ease and the least amount of stress. You take time to pack your bags and make sure you have everything you need, so if you encounter a detour or a bump in the road, you will know what to do. When building Your Mid-Career GPS, I find that many people rush through this all-important step and jump right into the logistics of finding their next job. I can't think of a bigger mistake.

In this chapter, you will:

- Learn why owning where you are and listening to your thoughts is vital to helping you prepare for this journey.
- Identify what's making you feel stuck in your career and how to appreciate your professional struggle.
- Assess "job fit" and how your attitudes help or hurt you in the job search process.
- Examine your professional strengths and explore how you do or don't use them in your current role.
- Acknowledge "fear of missing out" (i.e., FOMO) and Imposter Syndrome in your job search.
- Determine how your top five stories will help you get people interested in who you are and what you do.
- Identify the five influencers in your job search.
- Explore if now is the right time to apply for a new position.

Taking ownership of where you are in your career is vital. Right now, something is making you question a career move. You may be unhappy with your job. Perhaps you are unhappy with where you are working. Maybe you wonder how you can achieve a better work-life balance and still get to do work you love. For some of you, you may be working for a boss you don't like. And for others, you may be nearing retirement and trying to figure out what is the next, or final move, to get you across that finish line.

You have been listening to that little voice inside of your head, and on some days, it's pretty loud. That little voice has been keeping you up at night and making you question whether or not now is the right time for you to look for a new job.

We all have an inner voice or inner critic, and you must acknowledge it because it's trying to tell you something. That voice is causing you to wrestle with the following questions:

- What's working in your current position?
- What's not working in your current position?
- What do you like about your current position?
- What don't you like about your current position?
- What do you like about working for your current organization?
- What do you hate about working for your current organization?

- How much do you like your coworkers?
- How happy are you with your current salary or compensation structure?

My clients often breathe a sigh of relief when I bring up salary. It's almost as if they feel guilty talking about the money they are making or want to make. Let's be clear. Getting paid what you are worth and the value you bring to an organization is nothing to be ashamed of. Money lets us do things. Money allows us to honor our responsibilities, pay our bills, feed our families, donate to our favorite charities, enjoy our entertainment and recreation, and save for retirement. If you are unhappy with the amount of money you are making, own that. Making more money is never a bad thing if that is what you want.

As you build Your Mid-Career GPS, acknowledge that your career is a direct reflection of the totality of all your experiences. Those experiences make up the value and skill set you bring to your current position and a new organization. Acknowledging you are unhappy and wanting something more in your career is the first step.

What's Making You Unhappy in Your Career?

Work isn't always the happiest place to be. It can be challenging and frustrating. Sometimes, after you've been told your budget is being cut or you have to work with a difficult client or team member, it can make you unhappy. And when you are unhappy about work, it might keep you up at night. We spend the majority of our days at work. You know what is stressing you out, and you know what is causing you to be frustrated at the end of the day.

In her Flexjobs article, "4 Common Reasons to Change Careers," Christine Bernier references "career satisfaction, unsatisfactory leadership, work flexibility, and changing philosophies and goals" as the most common reasons people seek to change careers. Perhaps your primary motivation is on that list and it may give you a sense of validation. If your primary motive is not, that's okay too. As you create Your Mid-Career GPS, it is essential to identify what is pushing your buttons and causing you to be unhappy.

What's Making You Feel Stuck?

There is a difference between **feeling** stuck and **knowing** you are stuck. Having experienced this several times in my career, feeling stuck is one of the worst feelings. If you are feeling unhappy, there are things you can do to increase your overall job satisfaction. But suppose you are feeling stuck, meaning that you believe you are undervalued in your present organization, and you have received feedback stating there is no way for you to move forward. In that case, it probably feels as if you are left on an island to die.

When feeling stuck, how much of that is in your control? As companies re-organize, you may have landed in a less than optimal place on the org chart. If there are no opportunities for you to stretch, grow, be mentored, or work on a passion project that will help the organization, and you are told just to do your job, then, my friend, you are stuck. While there are benefits to having a steady job and a steady paycheck, this wears away fast when your career satisfaction plummets to an all-time low.

There is a difference between
feeling stuck and **knowing** you are stuck.

Adunola Adeshola's article for Forbes, "Feeling Stuck In Your Career? Do This First," outlines a three-step process to help you become "unstuck." Her first step is to declutter. Here, you identify what is making you feel stuck. Adeshola comments that saying "I feel stuck" is easy, but it doesn't require you to take any action. Her second step is to decide. Adeshola says, "Clarity comes from action, not thought. You can't think your way into clarity, so if you've been waiting to magically wake up one morning and feel unstuck, it's not going to happen. You have to make a decision." And lastly, "trust the process." I believe this is where having a defined career roadmap or GPS will help you get unstuck, take action, and get the results you want.

What is Your Professional Struggle?

Many of us struggled professionally because of COVID-19. When the NBA suspended their season due to a player testing positive for COVID-19, it was the beginning of an unprecedented life and career change. Short walks to another room in your house or apartment quickly replaced long commutes to work. For those who envisioned a glamorous life working from home, some quickly became disenfranchised and missed the camaraderie and collegiality of seeing their coworkers every day and the opportunity to connect with others in person.

In 2020, we saw record unemployment. We saw industries and businesses projecting record-breaking years, only to hemorrhage savings and for some, shut their doors. You watched your strategic plan and your professional goals come to a screeching halt, leaving you feeling heartbroken. It is one of the many reasons why I say that 2020 was an epic year. Our professional struggles took new meaning in 2020. We were given an opportunity to take a step back and reevaluate our personal and professional goals and dreams.

Megan Minutillo, the author of "Read This If You've Lost Sight Of Your Goals" for ThoughtCatalog.com, says, "To feel unfulfilled and purposeless can be disturbing, and heartbreaking, and paralyzing. And you're not alone in that. You're not crazy for feeling that way. Without a feeling purpose, we become susceptible to depression, and despair, and overwhelming negativity – and that's not a pleasant rabbit hole to fall down."

2020 was a year of immense professional and personal struggle. As you think about Your Mid-Career GPS, what happened that caused you to either get off track or double down your efforts in your career? Identifying your professional struggle is extremely important for Your Mid-Career GPS because it helps you tell your story more genuinely and authentically. To stand out from your competition, you do that by learning how to tell your story and communicate why a company needs to see the value in who you are and what you do.

For those who are currently unemployed or furloughed, know that many people have career gaps. Some gaps are created by choice, such as to raise a family or take care of aging parents, and others are due to circumstances where companies downsize or cut costs, and unfortunately, you were let go. These gaps are part of your story. You should not run or shy away from talking about these gaps.

When I graduated college, I remember a career advisor telling me that the last thing I would ever want on my résumé is a gap. A gap, or break in employment, meant that I was an undesirable employee or not valuable. I remember that scaring the hell out of me. I also remember that when I "was let go from a job," my heart sank into my stomach. I had the gap on my résumé, and it became part of my story. When people asked me about it, I acknowledged the events and moved the conversation into my value and how I could help them.

Undeniably one of the most challenging groups hit by 2020 has been women. In her article for Fool.com titled, "COVID-19 Is Driving Women Out of the Workforce," Maurie Backman talks about the impact the pandemic has had on women and why they have been the ones who took the step back and sacrificed their careers. Maurie writes, "But right now, a lot of women's hands are tied. Those who can't work remotely may have to take time out of the workforce to watch their children and guide them in virtual learning – a set up many school districts have adapted to kick off the 2020-2021 academic year. While it may be possible to find childcare in creative ways – signing up for learning pods or hiring sitters – in some cases, that's too cost-prohibitive to consider. Or, to put it another way, some women may be better off quitting their jobs and watching their children, rather than spending the bulk of their earnings – or even more than their earnings – on child care."

Your professional struggle is real, and it is a part of your story. You get to choose how much of your struggle helps you or holds you back from creating whatever is next for your career. Nevertheless, I sincerely hope that hiring managers and employers look at what's happened in 2020 and the decisions you made as necessary and a direct statement about your personal and professional values. If they don't, you probably don't want to work there anyway.

Career Paths Are Messy and Your GPS Will Get You to Your Next Career Destination

Career paths are messy. If you think your career path is supposed to be perfectly linear, I'm here to tell you that you are completely misguided. Somewhere we believed that everything is supposed to work out "perfectly." The reality is everyone's career path has some kind of detour, bump, exit, hurdle, or struggle along the way. No one ever said your career path was going to be easy. Honestly, I'm grateful my career path is a little messy. I wouldn't be able to do the work I get to do today if my career path was perfect and pristine.

Growing up, I was led to believe that when you landed an excellent job, you would stay in it for the rest of your career. My father was the primary breadwinner for my family, and he worked undeniably hard. He managed a service station on the New Jersey Turnpike. When the company he worked for lost their contract, he found himself studying vigorously for a new position within the organization. I remember him sitting at the kitchen table one evening voraciously studying blueprints to figure out where to move the oil when it came off the tanker to distribute at the refinery. This wasn't easy for him, but he studied endlessly to make sure he was prepared for the test and the interview. I asked him what would happen if he didn't get the job. He looked at me with these piercing eyes of his and very calmly and confidently said, "John, there is no other option. I have to get this job." My father got that job and stayed there for the remainder of his career until he retired. My father taught me one of his biggest lessons; to work hard, do quality work, and be a good person.

My father was a planner and didn't handle detours well. Change was hard for him. He took great pride in his work, and being told that he was losing his job at his age, I'm sure it scared him. While I wasn't old enough to be privy to late-night conversations he and my mother had about his job and his fears, he did what he needed to do to take care of his family and honor his responsibilities, even if it meant he wasn't the happiest all the time doing the work he did.

You are entirely responsible for your career and the decisions you make about it. This book is not designed or intended to cast judgment or champion a decision about whether or not you should stay in your current role or leave it. Accepting that your career path is messy is a great way to release the pressure that everything in your career has to be "perfect." Join the hundreds of millions of people who share something in common with you! At some point, everyone is trying to figure out what is next for them professionally, and that is why preparation is the key to creating Your Mid-Career GPS.

Listen to Your Inner Critic, but Decide about How Much You Trust It

We all have an inner voice that tells us what we should or shouldn't do. That voice is a voice of reason, protection, fear, and action. In my coaching practice, I help my clients listen very carefully to what their inner critic is saying to them by exploring their thoughts about what is next for them professionally. After all, your inner critic isn't your biggest cheerleader. It's protecting you from the things you are most fearful of or hesitant about as you create your next advancement opportunity.

I know that some people like to refer to their inner critic as their "gut." It is that part of them that is instinctual, and more often, their gut never steers them in the wrong direction. Yet, sometimes our inner critics can be harsh. It can say things that hold us back from taking action and going after what we want, even though it is trying to protect us.

Maybe your inner critic says you shouldn't apply to a particular job because you don't meet all the qualifications. Perhaps your inner critic is telling you not to waste your time applying for a position because you're not going to hear from them anyway. Spend some time answering these questions to help you listen to your inner critic:

When does your inner critic hold you
back from applying for a position?

When does your inner critic say to go for a
particular opportunity?

What does your inner critic say to you when everything is going well?

What does your inner critic say to you when you are under stress?

Our inner critics can limit us from going after what we want and tell us we are not worth trying to better ourselves. How many times have you talked yourself out of doing something, only to regret you didn't take the chance? Our inner critics can protect us from disappointment, fear, or getting hurt. For example, our inner critics may keep us from applying to a company we are interested in, or networking with someone who may be a great connection for us and vice versa. Our inner critics make us second guess our intentions by telling us we are not good enough or we shouldn't set ourselves up for potential disappointment. That's why having a GPS will help you keep your plan and strategy in place while navigating various career opportunities and challenges.

Navigating career transitions are scary. Our inner critics want to hold us back and keep us safe or comfortable in what's known or familiar. If you are considering asking your boss for a raise, your inner critic is likely telling you why you aren't good enough or not deserving of it, even though you've exceeded expectations. Lean in to what your inner critic is saying to you about a particular decision or circumstance. Our inner critics love to make us second guess our intentions. Be clear about what you want. Set that professional destination into your GPS and then get to work following it.

How Do You Know When It's Time to Leave Your Job?

There is truth in the adage, "the best time to find a job is when you have one." We know that this doesn't always happen. As evident in 2020, you may have been laid off or furloughed from a job you loved and found yourself trying to figure out what to do next.

As I shared with you earlier, some stressors help you determine how likely you are to stay in your present job. If there are things or circumstances that make you unhappy, it is time for you to actively consider whether or not you want to invest the time, energy, and money to make a career change.

In her article for The Balanced Careers, Alison Doyle outlines various "Signs It's Time to Quit Your Job." Doyle shares these "warning signs" that make sense as we consider whatever is next. Many years ago, one of my coaches shared with me that there is a difference between "having to do" something versus "getting to do something."

When we "get" to do something, we do it because it is a choice. We are excited about doing that activity. When we "have" to do something, we are doing it out of a sense of obligation. There will be times throughout your career when you feel you "have" to go to work. Not every day is a picnic. In part, that's what makes it work. You know when you enjoy your work, the people you work with, the people you help, and where you work. Thus, your outlook or attitudes about your job are far more positive.

According to many job search experts and Alison Doyle, there are many hints or signs when you are thinking about leaving your job. Some of these might include procrastinating or dreading going to work, feeling like you are professionally stuck, or experiencing what I call a "values conflict" where you don't feel professionally aligned to the company's mission or vision. Your instinct will tell you when you are unhappy in your job. So it's important to listen to it.

How many of these warning signs have you experienced in your career? I've experienced practically all of them, and I agree with Alison Doyle that they are valid reasons for looking for a new job. When building Your Mid-Career GPS, these considerations occur in this Prepare phase. Without this phase, you are merely throwing spaghetti at the wall to see if it sticks.

I'm going to share with you three monumental events that have happened in my career. Early in my career, my contract was "not renewed." Now, this is a nice way of saying "you're fired," but you still need to finish your contract. I'll admit it wasn't easy SHOWing UP to work every day for the next four months, knowing that I had a definitive end date. Sometimes our employers give us a heads up that either our contract isn't going to be renewed or we are in jeopardy of being terminated. It is vital to listen to those conversations and figure out what action steps you want to take. These aren't easy conversations to have – whether you are giving them or receiving them – but they are pivotal along your career journey.

Fast forward almost 25 years, and I found myself working for a wonderful organization but stuck in a dead-end position. I loved the people I was working with, and for the most part, I loved the work I was doing. But wanting to do something more was not an option for me in that organization. In one of the most memorable and most meaningful conversations I have ever had with a superior, I asked my boss directly for confirmation that my career path was, at best, horizontal. When she confirmed that my thoughts were correct, I knew what was going to be next. I had spent the better part of six months planning and strategizing what it would look like to pursue an entrepreneurial path and launch my coaching practice full time. This was not an easy decision. Many sleepless nights and multiple conversations with myself in the car as I was driving home from work led me to have a conversation with my husband about whether we could support me leaving my job and pursuing this entrepreneurial route. I could've stayed doing the job I was assigned to do. I would have worked alongside some wonderful people and clients and been utterly miserable, feeling unsatisfied and unfulfilled, knowing I was capable of doing far more than what I was assigned. And while I was not at risk of getting fired, I also knew that where I had landed on the organizational chart meant that I wasn't in the most optimal place and could very easily be seen as an expense that could be cut. I will always be grateful I wasn't let go from that job.

After much deliberation and conversations with my husband, my career coach, and myself, I decided to leave my job. Hands down it is probably the gutsiest move I have ever made in my career, and I don't regret it one bit. Sometimes, our career roadmap takes us to a place where we stare at a fork in the road and decide which way to go. It may not be the easiest road to take, but I can tell you, I'm the happiest I have ever been in my career. And I've held some wonderful jobs.

Lastly, a young woman who directly reported to me came into my office one day, clearly feeling frustrated and disappointed in where her career was going inside the organization. I knew that she was highly talented and was underpaid for what she was doing. Yet, according to her salary band, she was paid moderately well for where she was in the organization. We were having one of our regularly scheduled check-in meetings when she looked at me and told me that she could get paid double what she was doing elsewhere. I looked at her, and I said, "You're right. How do I help you leave?" She looked at me with a stunned expression on her face, as if she couldn't believe what I was saying. I looked at her and said again, "How do I help you leave? Your talents can be used far better elsewhere, so as your boss, how do I help you achieve that goal?"

Now, I knew as her boss, where I was limited in how much she could be paid or what title she could have. She and I were on the same page in knowing that her best move was to leave, but her surprised look on her face caught me once again.

Then, I looked at her and said, "Oh! Did you think that you could come to my office, tell me you could get paid double elsewhere, and I would just give you more money?" She put her head down ever so slightly. I reminded her that there were times when we as employees may make such a play. However, to do this most effectively, you need to make sure you have a backup plan. She didn't have one, but I was willing to help her create one. What happened in the next 45 minutes was nothing short of a life-changing moment for her career. We scripted a roadmap that included where she wanted to work, what she wanted to do, what degree she needed to have, and how she would go about doing that. We also laid out a time frame that took several years to accomplish everything we outlined in her professional GPS. She left my office with a plan. For me, as her manager, I had a development plan for her as well. She was one of those "high performing" young professionals who are destined to do remarkable things, but it wasn't likely going to happen in that job in that organization. Over the next three years, she executed that plan flawlessly. Not only did she find a fantastic new job and the salary she wanted, but also she discovered ways to grow in that new organization. I am undeniably proud of her for how she SHOWs UP each day to do the work she has been called to do.

Deciding to leave your job is personal. Be very careful who you tell or who you solicit for feedback or guidance. Keep that circle small and only include the people you trust. Often, we make the mistake of seeking input from more people to validate what we are thinking. Find those critical friends who will give you the honest and truthful advice you need. They will serve you well in creating Your Mid-Career GPS.

Leaving your job is like taking a detour. While not planned, it's a path to help you reach your destination without sitting in a lot of traffic and getting frustrated. Sometimes detours save us time, gets us there safely, and avoids a lot of stress.

I know that you will determine when the best time is for you to leave your job. These decisions are yours and yours alone. After months and months of deliberation, I finally was ready to launch my coaching practice full-time and notify my employer I was leaving. I will never forget the look on my husband's face when he told me that he had promised himself he would never tell me to quit my job, but there were about three times when he came close. He said he couldn't stand to see me as stressed and frustrated as I was, but he knew I had to reach that decision myself. He couldn't pressure me, and he vowed he wouldn't make this decision for me. I will always be eternally grateful to him for that and many other things.

The Goal – Finding a Job You Love or Loving the Job You Have

As you set out to create Your Mid-Career GPS, know that the ultimate goal is to find a job that you love or love the job you have. You are embarking on a mission to increase your job satisfaction. Creating Your Mid-Career GPS is about helping you figure out what is next. At this point, we are making no promises – meaning we are not putting weight on one outcome over another. You will get to figure out whatever is next. Trust that if you do the work, you are going to be okay and better yourself. This process has helped many of my clients explore and examine what's next for them and their careers.

You are embarking on a mission
to increase your job satisfaction.
Creating Your Mid-Career GPS is about
helping you figure out what is next.

Assessing Where You Are and What "Fit" Looks Like

My clients are concerned and want to know what "fit" looks like for them in their careers. When I ask them to define what "fit" is, I get many different answers. For some, it has to do with aligning their values to a new organization. For others, it is about finding a job that is going to be fulfilling and rewarding. But "fit" is all about that special something that only you can define. It's probably easier for you to know when a job doesn't "fit" than when it does. "Fit" feels like you are driving at 65 mph, or 75 mph depending on where you live, and there is no traffic for miles. You have a clear path toward your destination and you love that feeling.

Defining what "fit" looks like is an integral part of the preparation phase in creating Your Mid-Career GPS. It is something that can easily be overlooked because you think you know what it is. The coaching questions I ask my clients are important for determining what kinds of positions and organizations they will look at when searching for a new job.

For example, ask yourself:
- What has made you incredibly happy in your career?
- What would make you incredibly happy in your career now?
- What would it be like having the most fantastic boss you've ever had in your career?
- What would it feel like to have a team that always has your back and collaborates like no other team you have worked with to make results happen?
- What does the organizational culture feel like in a new workplace?
- How closely must your personal and professional values align with the organization's values?
- How much required travel are you willing to do?

- How much responsibility do you want?
- What's the least amount of money you are willing to make in this new position?

And once you land that new job, you might wonder how long this "fit" will last. There is no way to answer that. There are times when we love our jobs and other times when we don't. A dear friend and mentor told me that I could think of my time in thirds at a particular organization. There will be a third of the time when I loved what I was doing. There will be a third of the time when I will hate it. And there will be a third of the time when it seems as if I'm just hanging out in the middle and going through the motions. He said if you have that kind of career here, you've done pretty well for yourself. He encouraged me to set clear and realistic expectations for what I was looking for in this job, and to be open and honest with myself about when they were met or not.

Finding the right fit, and maintaining it within any organization, takes about as much work as it does with any relationship. You have to do the work. You have to be prepared to SHOW UP and have intentional conversations when necessary to get the information you need to make the best decisions for your career. If you can find a job where you "fit," then I believe you've done pretty well for yourself. It is okay if your definition of "fit" changes over time and changes across various organizations. The point is, you must honor when the work you are doing fits and when it does not.

How Your Attitudes Help You or Hurt You in Your Job Search

When I work with a client, I begin by using a powerful assessment tool called the Energy Leadership Index™ (ELI). I became a Master Practitioner in administering the Energy Leadership Index™ through the Institute for Professional Excellence in Coaching. The ELI gives the client information about the attitudes or lenses they place on situations when they perform at their best and when they are under stress. During your career transition, you are experiencing many emotions. Increasing your attitudinal awareness is one data point to determine how you can build your GPS to get you to your next position.

In my practice, I've seen how mid-career professionals resonate with the ELI's information because they have enough experience to recognize how their attitudes may affect how they

SHOW UP in their careers. This is a different way to approach your mid-career transition rather than jumping into updating your résumé. Being clear about your attitudes help you understand what influencers or stressors affect your career happiness and decisions. Increasing your attitudinal awareness may help you avoid moving into a new job with the same kind of stressors you've had in the past. This is about making a change that you believe will increase your overall job satisfaction and help you make a more significant impact.

Let's create a Pro/Con List of the things you do and don't want in a new position. In the Pro column, write down all of the things you want in a new job. Then, write down all of the things you don't want in the Con column.

To download your free Pro/Con List, visit https://johnneral.com

Pro	#	Con	#
Total		Total	

Once you've created your list, go back and assign a point value to each item in the appropriate column ranging from 1 to 5. Be very specific when rating each item. Don't assign everything a "3" because you can't decide how important it is. Be clear about what is a "5," "4," and so on. Once you have a value assigned to each item in your pro/con list, go ahead and tally up each side's score. While this is unscientific, it will give you some data to reflect upon as to whether or not a particular job, organization, or opportunity is right for you at this time.

If you don't do this work, you gloss over everything to consider when it comes to a new job. You may intentionally overlook some qualities or responsibilities that could be stressful for you with the new position. For example, you may not want a long commute. If there are no other job opportunities, you may decide that having a longer commute is acceptable for right now. I have seen this happen with clients wrestling with specific opportunities or even in terms of how much travel they would have – understandably pre-pandemic. You want clarity on the attitudes or lenses you are placing on any new opportunity. Later in the book, when we start addressing networking and interviewing, this will help determine what questions you want to ask to get all of the information you need to help you decide what's next for Your Mid-Career GPS.

To learn more about the Energy Leadership Index™, visit https://energyleadership.com.

What Are Your Strengths and How Are You Using Them (or Not) in Your Current Role?

The second assessment I use with my clients is Gallup's CliftonStrengths Assessment. Gallup uses 34 different workplace strengths and finds that when someone can use their dominant workplace strengths, they tend to experience greater job satisfaction and happiness. This assessment will help you unlock a deeper understanding of where you are strongest, help you work better with others, and help you gain clarity about where you are most valuable.

I remember my boss asking me to decide between two roles in an organization. One was very people-focused. I would help manage a relatively large team and develop their talent across multiple projects. The downside to this position was that it would be difficult to determine how effective I was in this role, and it wasn't directly responsible for generating revenue. The other role was more project based and client focused. It also was directly responsible for generating revenue for the company by managing a multi-million-dollar project. Knowing my strengths, I chose the more people-centric position. To own where I was and deliver the most value, then my management skills, along with my ability to provide effective professional development, were more valuable than me leading a project.

As you chart a path toward whatever is next for you professionally, I encourage you to think about what you are and are not good at. Your talents or strengths are needed in many organizations. It's your job – no pun intended – to figure out where you can do your best work and who needs your talents right now. That's why knowing your strengths is crucial to determining what is your best "fit.". Taking this assessment will provide you with a wealth of information. It can almost be too much information, but I find that to be a good thing. This assessment gives the client plenty of information to examine and explore where they are using, or not using, their strengths in their current role.

If you'd like to learn more about the Gallup Clifton StrengthsFinder Assessment, visit https://www.gallup.com and search for Clifton Strengths.

Why You Worry About FOMO

By its definition, Google says that FOMO is "the anxiety that an exciting or interesting event may currently be happening elsewhere, often aroused by posts seen on social media." FOMO plays a role in creating Your Mid-Career GPS.

Imagine hearing about or seeing a job posted online. You frantically get everything to apply because you do not want to miss out on that opportunity. That's fine, but let's acknowledge this is one way FOMO presents itself in your job search. It's like cutting across four lanes of traffic to get to the exit because you found your favorite fast food restaurant at that exit and don't want to miss out on that <insert favorite snack here>.

Be careful when FOMO presents itself. As part of your preparation in developing Your Mid-Career GPS, make sure you intentionally apply for positions you see as a great fit. FOMO may cause us to apply for everything. Let's be clear. You are taking intentional steps to create whatever is next for your career. Make sure you are directing your efforts and energy in the places you see best.

Who Are You Trying to Emulate? (Imposter Syndrome)

Imposter Syndrome is real and is found in many areas of your personal and professional lives. It exists in all industries and organizations. I've seen it in all of my clients because they want to do their best. I've personally experienced it as well.

According to CareerFoundry, in their article, "58% of Tech Employees Experience Imposter

Syndrome. Here's How to Overcome It," "Imposter syndrome was first documented in the '70s in reference to successful working women who believed that they somehow fooled everyone around them into thinking they were intelligent, despite receiving professional recognition in their field and garnering respect from colleagues. Since then, it's become an epidemic across multiple industries – particularly in business and tech circles. The definition of imposter syndrome has also expanded to encompass people of any gender."

We all experience Imposter Syndrome. Just look at the "Perfect Family Photos" or "Perfect Bodies" on social media, and you can quickly start feeling as if you are missing out on something.

Sure, someone is always going to be better than you or make more money than you. Someone is always going to be promoted quicker than you. And if you are thinking that about someone else, rest assured someone is thinking the same thing about you. Imposter syndrome is a vicious cycle. The sooner we break free from it, put it in its place, and set ground rules for how we want to SHOW UP in our career as authentically and genuinely as possible, the better off we will be.

CareerFoundry goes on to say, "People who suffer from imposter syndrome perpetuate the notion that they have to work extra hard to achieve success, rather than attributing their success to their natural talent. They do double the work as their peers to prove that they are worthy of being there. The result? A working life riddled with anxiety, exhaustion, and potentially even resulting in major burnout. This is particularly relevant in the tech industry, where its fast-paced and dynamic nature means many feel pressured to perform better than anyone else in order to stay in their jobs."

With record unemployment and increased competition for jobs in 2020, many people allowed Imposter Syndrome to dominate their job search, networking, and interview process. Be who you are. Focus on how you can add the most value to a new organization because of what you do and how you plan to SHOW UP for it. Your knowledge and skill set are a vital currency in the marketplace.

Think about how much time you waste trying to be someone else. These are the exact lessons we learned on the elementary school playground. Yet, as adults, we still find ourselves trying to learn these lessons. When you think about overcoming imposter syndrome, I invite you to remember your skills. Focus on what you have done and what you are learning. Find a mentor or trusted colleague who can answer questions about your career path when things arise for you.

Nothing is ever going to be perfect. Our careers are messy. The sooner you acknowledge that, the quicker you will get out of your own way, and the better off you will be. Set the ground rule now that you focus solely on who you are as a professional and the value you bring better than anyone else in your organization or to a future company. This way, your thoughts are solely focused inward, controlling what you can do, what you are learning, and what you are responsible for, rather than focusing on what someone else is doing.

Set the ground rule now that you focus solely on who you are as a professional and the value you bring better than anyone else in your organization or to a future company.

Battling Ageism at Every Point in Your Career

Ageism exists at every stage in our careers. Early on, when you wanted to move up the ladder as quickly as possible, you may have heard that you were too young or didn't have enough experience. Thus, your young age was a perception that someone may have used against you to determine whether or not you were best suited for a particular position. When I work with people who are just entering mid-career, they are inclined to view themselves as still being in their "early-career" rather than highlighting the value they bring to a new position.

As we get older, we may wish for those younger days. There are so many articles and research about how to combat ageism. I must acknowledge that ageism is real, and it is a shame. The fact that someone would make a judgment about your abilities or value as a professional solely because of your age - whether you are younger or older - is shameful. Sadly, we must find ways to combat ageism wherever possible.

The website Celarity cites "8 Ways to Combat Ageism While Searching for a Job." There are some great tips I want to reference here to help you take the focus off of your age and shift attention to the value you'll bring to a new organization. We will talk more about these in a later section, but it is worth mentioning here because it's integral to how we prepare ourselves in the job search.

Celarity mentions things such as:

- Have a professional-looking email address from a current provider. For example, using an email address from a server no one has heard about in years may put you at a disadvantage.
- Take all graduation dates off your résumé. This is an essential tip for professionals at any age because it automatically makes someone begin to decipher how old you are and make a judgment about you.
- Your résumé is a marketing tool to highlight your value. While we will discuss this later in the positioning chapter, a general rule of thumb is not to go over 15 years on a chronological résumé.
- Showcase your ability to adapt to a variety of situations, such as learning current technology. This has been especially true as a result of 2020. We saw an uptick in online learning platforms such as LinkedIn Learning and Coursera, where people were

using their time during quarantine to learn new skills they could apply to new positions.

- Network. There is power in having a network that will help and support you by making meaningful connections and providing valuable resources when needed. Build and grow your network intentionally.

- Your experience is an advantage. Coaching my clients on how to tell their story from a place of value and service is one of the most significant components of our time together. An excellent hiring manager is going to know whether you genuinely believe your story or not. If you have the experience, appreciate and showcase it.

What Are Your Top Five Career Experiences or Accomplishments?

As part of your preparation, begin to make a list of your top five career experiences or accomplishments. This will help you communicate your value whether you are networking, being interviewed, writing your résumé, or optimizing your LinkedIn profile. Where you are right now is because of the totality of your personal and professional experiences. To tell your story effectively, you must cherish and own each experience and accomplishment.

To help you prepare for what is coming up in this book, write down five positive career experiences or accomplishments you believe will help you tell your career story at a networking event or interview.

My Top Five Career Experiences or Accomplishments
1.
2.
3.
4.
5.

Why is There Power in the Pivot?

A pivot is about making a change. For example, you may be looking to secure an internal promotion or leave your current organization by leveraging your talent and expertise. You may also look to do something completely different. You may decide to go back to school and pursue an additional degree. You may even consider an entrepreneurial journey.

Pivots help us stretch and grow. A few years ago, my husband, my best friend from college, and I took an adventure through the Midwest. We spent a lot of time in the car and saw some incredible and beautiful places in our country. One of the highlights of our trip was visiting Yellowstone National Park.

When we checked into our room, we learned there was a power outage inside the park. We were all excited. Sure there were some minor inconveniences, but we weren't there for the electricity. We were there for the experience – to see the beauty that Yellowstone has to offer.

We saw people visibly upset that their dinner reservations weren't going to happen or wondering how they would spend their evenings with no electricity. You're in Yellowstone. Get over it!

We quickly devised a plan to grab some sandwiches and drinks and ventured into the park before getting too dark and then safely getting back to our rooms. Sitting in our rooms with no electricity and watching the sun go down, I observed the darkness in the park increase over a few minutes into something I will never forget. In all of Yellowstone's majesty, there was this quiet. It was breathtaking. It wasn't until 10 o'clock that evening when the power came back on. We took time to charge our devices and get ready for an early start the next day so we could greet the sunrise in Yellowstone.

I treasure that event because had I allowed myself to get caught up in all of the stress and fight the situation in front of us, I would never have experienced everything I did that evening. To this day, it is still one of the most memorable parts of our trip. Fighting the pivot would've been a waste of energy. Fighting the career pivot is also a massive waste of energy.

What is a Career Pivot?

"Many people hit a plateau in their careers and feel an inexplicable urge to do things differently. The way they have been working is no longer working for them," says Jenny Blake, author of "Pivot: The Only Move That Matters is the Next One." Think of the pivot as a shift. You are shifting into something that is going to serve you better in the next moment.

Kit Warchol, in her article for Skillcrush.com titled, "How to Make a Career Pivot: The Ultimate No B.S. Guide," states, "a career Pivot usually aligns with a pivotal moment in your life and work, one where you have the choice to stay with the status quo or take a measured rest to increase your career pace."

How Do I Not Make a Mistake? Follow Your GPS!

I hear this question a lot from my coaching clients. It's understandable that as you decide to make a career change, the last thing you want to do is screw up. Where is the pressure coming from? Is the pressure coming solely from you, or is there someone close to you putting pressure on you to make sure that this career move is the "right" one?

You have an excellent opportunity to think about what thoughts you are putting in your head. When making a career change or finding a new opportunity, it's all about your mindset. How you want to SHOW UP at this moment is entirely based on your thoughts. You get to make a choice here. You can choose to "play full out," or you can decide to hold everything back for fear that you are going to make a tremendous mistake.

When thinking about what's next for your career, how likely is it that you would actually "fail" or "make a huge mistake?" The likelihood is, you won't. I have never met anyone who considered making a career move and intentionally said, "I want to screw up." Your brain will play some tricks on you and do what it can to protect you from any pain or harm in the job search and life.

I'll share more with you later in the book about "being tied to the outcome." For now, I want you to focus on the thoughts you have about this career move and whether you are building yourself up or taking yourself out of contention.

Why You Need to Be Great at Telling Your Story

When people inquire about how I can help them as their career coach, they tell me they are not good at "selling themselves." If there is one common theme or characteristic across all of my clients, they are very heart-centered professionals who don't like talking about themselves. After all, I don't work with cold-hearted people.

Heart-centered leaders and professionals typically struggle to sell themselves or find ways to genuinely and authentically tell their stories because their default is to focus on others. To turn the attention or the spotlight on themselves often makes them very uncomfortable. It's why they typically struggle with the "tell me about yourself" question during an interview, and it's one of the biggest things that we work on during coaching.

In her article "21 Unmistakable Traits of a Heart-Centered Leader" for Inc.com, Susan Steinbrecher writes, "In essence, heart-centered leadership is not a singular gold standard or an ultimate pinnacle that only a rare few can achieve. It lies in your ability to stop, go inward, and reflect on the course of action that you know is the right one rather than succumbing to external pressures and circumstances. Leading from the heart is not just a nice idea or theory or some magical dream. By embracing a heart-centered approach to leadership, you will be in a more powerful position than you could have imagined."

Heart-centered leaders and professionals thrive when given the opportunities to serve their organizations, clients, and teams. Often, these professionals will stay in a job longer than they desire because they genuinely enjoy the people they work with or have a great client, and they don't want to leave them. These behaviors put them second because they are so focused on everyone else. The goal is to honor what they need for themselves and their careers at this moment.

What holds you back from sharing your value, your talents, and your expertise? It's time to get out of the slow lane while you let everyone pass you, and move into the fast lane to start telling your story differently than you've ever done. People need to hear it, and honestly, they want to listen to it. This is why preparing for your next career move is vital to Your Mid-Career GPS.

As I mentioned earlier, you need to have five relevant accomplishments or experiences that will help you tell your story. Your stories need to be centered on the value you have brought to that position. Even if it is under your leadership, you must take ownership of what you directly created or led because that is part of your value.

We know that standardized testing is a big deal. As a teacher, it was always a huge focus each year to ensure our students were more than prepared for the test. One year, we created these "Test Prep Fridays" where we would only focus on test preparation to help ease our students' anxiety and help them be more prepared for the test. You and

I know that putting a spotlight on things doesn't always make it easier. In fact, it can dramatically increase someone's anxiety and put undue pressure on them.

One year, I decided to forego the "Test Prep Fridays" and do what I did best - teach an excellent curriculum that would more than adequately prepare my students for the state test. I ditched the worksheets and the "test prep" exercises, and I taught the standards. My job was to teach the curriculum. That's what I did.

When test day came, I knew I had done everything I could to prepare my students for the test, and they were ready. Months later, when the assessment results were released, 100% of my students passed the assessment.

I remember being called into the superintendent's office to celebrate my students' success. I was asked how the "Test Prep Fridays" went and why I thought they were so beneficial to helping my students pass the state assessment. Now, I'm sure you can imagine the look of surprise on my superintendent's face when I told him that I didn't do any of it. I looked at him and said, "I taught our curriculum. It's more than enough." He was surprised and a bit dismayed that I didn't follow a directive as I have always been compliant. It was a great learning opportunity for all of us, and honestly, we did less and less test prep after that – or at least we changed our view on it.

That was one of my five stories and I became really good at telling it. Every interview, conference, and networking opportunity I had, I would share that story, and it generated a lot of interest and discussion about what we were doing in my district. That's why it's vital to get really good at telling your story from a place of value and service. People will want to know more.

How Will You Manage Your Stress in the Job Search?

We all handle stress differently. By now, you have probably adopted or integrated particular stress-reducing techniques to help manage it daily. I don't have any earth-shattering or revolutionary techniques or tricks to help you manage your stress or energy during this job search process.

I know from working with my clients that their knowledge of the Energy Leadership Index ™ and the information in the Energetic Self-Perception

Chart ™ helps them be more aware of and manage their stress or shift their energy when they need it. This is particularly beneficial in the coaching relationship because we often discuss where they are energetically and how that affects their stress.

SHOW UP from a place of competence, confidence, value, and service.

But if there is one tip I can share with you to help you manage your stress in the job search process, it is this. SHOW UP from a place of competence, confidence, value, and service. In reading this book, you are increasing your competence to figure out your next career move. Additionally, you are building your confidence by reading this book and talking to people you trust about whether you are ready to make this next move. And lastly, throughout my life and career, I have found that it reduces most of the stress when I come from a place of value and service. You will never go wrong if you are adding value and leading with your heart.

What Are the Five Influencers in Your Job Search?

Five influencers will affect your job search. These influencers are things that you will strongly consider when deciding what jobs to apply for. These influencers will affect your final decision regarding which position you ultimately take. These influencers are:

1. Physical – Every job has its physical demands. Examine the labor intensity of the job. Additionally, you will consider your commuting time, how much you will be standing or sitting during the day, and lifting objects, for example.
2. Emotional – What is the emotional toll this job will have on you? How much emotional stress will you endure? For example, some sales positions are compensated solely based on how much product you sell in a given month. Some people thrive in this kind of situation, and others worry about the lack of a consistent paycheck every two weeks. Ultimately, you will decide how much emotional stress you are willing to take with a new position.
3. Intellectual – How much intellectual activity will you have on this job? How

much will you use your knowledge, experiences, and skill set in this new position? How much does this new position address your key strengths you learned from the Gallup Clifton StrengthsFinder Assessment?

4. Financial – Money matters. How much you are paid for the work you will do must align with your expectations and what you believe you are worth in that role.

5. Relationship – All jobs take a toll on our relationships. How will this new job potentially affect your relationship? Are the demands of the position going to be so much that your spouse or partner will wish you were home more often or not working as hard? Will the demands of the new job improve your relationship?

These influencers are essential to consider when preparing for what's next. These questions are mulling in your head anyway. If they are not, then I encourage you to reflect on these influencers and the impact they are going to have on your decision. Remember, in the preparation stage, we are exploring all options. Nothing is off the table. Consider how a new position may affect your professional and personal life.

Why is Now the Right Time to Apply for a New Position?

Clients ask me if now is the right time for them to apply for a new position and whether or not they should take the risk in applying. It's not for me to say. As a coach, my ethical responsibility is to help my clients explore their thoughts and potential actions to create their best plan. As their coach, I advocate, champion, and challenge them so they can explore their options. Coaching is a judgment-free experience. Granted, I may hold up the proverbial mirror and show them their self-judgment and how it is affecting their decisions. But as their coach, I have no vested interest in whatever they decide is next for their career. We build our working relationship on the principle that they will make the best decision for themselves.

If you are wondering if now is the right time to apply for a new position, I invite you to clarify your reasons why you believe now is the time to take action. Notice I didn't say the "best" time. Your reasons will determine your level of intensity and commitment to this process. Are you all in or not?

What is your timeline for securing a new position? For some of you, the answer was yesterday! And while that can't happen, your urgency is understood and appreciated. For others, the timeline might be a little longer. Write down how long you believe it is going to take you to find a new position. Then, double that timeline and ask yourself, "If you were to find a new job in that amount of time, would you be okay with it?"

In 2020, many people experienced longer than desired timelines for finding a new job. I have had clients who heard crickets for months, only to receive multiple emails and phone calls with invitations to interviews that led to numerous job offers several months, or even a year, later. The market and industry will always dictate how long it will take you to find a job. However, your commitment to taking action and effort in this process will always be the one thing you can control.

The market and industry will always dictate
how long it will take you to find a job.
However, your commitment to taking action
and effort in this process will always be the
one thing you can control.

This has been and will always be a numbers game.
And while some applicants will apply for one job
and receive an offer, many others will invest
months, sending dozens of résumés and
applications to be offered only one interview. If
you are looking to create optimal results, then you
must have optimal commitment. You cannot apply
to one to three jobs a week and expect great
results. If that happens to you from only applying
to one to three jobs a week, I am thrilled for you.
The more positions you identify that closely align
with what you want during this preparation stage,
the more likely you will get an interview.

I strongly suggest you use some kind of job search
tracker. I like to use Excel or Google Sheets. At a
minimum, that tracker must list the company's
name, its website, a point of contact (if possible)
and their email address, the link to the job posting,

the date you applied, and the date you heard from them. You can visit https://johnneral.com to download a free tracker to help you organize your job search efforts better. Additionally, you will want to track any dates where you were invited for an interview and when that interview occurred. Failure to track this data allows you to embellish or lie to yourself about how many jobs you have looked at and applied for. You will also want to capture any notes you have regarding conversations with people inside the company or organization and your actions.

We will talk about networking in an upcoming chapter, but I want to emphasize that your ability to leverage your network in the job search process is vital to your success. According to Julia Freeland Fisher in her CNBC article, "How to Get a Job Often Comes Down to One Elite Personal Asset, and Many People Still Don't Realize It," "as much as 80% of jobs are filled through personal and professional connections." Start talking to people you know and trust about where you are headed and see how they can help you.

If you take the time to do this preparation work, I can guarantee you that it makes your career transition much more manageable. There are reasons why this process helps my clients take action, rather than merely updating their résumé and applying for positions.

In the next stage, I will show you what it means to position yourself accordingly in your career transition and how the positioning stage is where you will take massive action to help you create your next advancement opportunity on Your Mid-Career GPS.

Why is now the right time for you to begin a job search and apply for new positions?

What are some of your "must haves" for a new job to feel as if it is the right "fit"?

What are your best professional strengths?

Why would someone want you in their organization?

Chapter 2

Position – Let's Strategically Plan How to Get There

————————

In the last section, you spent time getting ready and preparing for your journey. You focused on exploring your attitudes, strengths, and value so you could own where you are, assess your current career trajectory, and determine what steps you want to take. We talked about FOMO and Imposter Syndrome and how those things are either helping you or holding you back from getting in the fast lane and heading toward your destination. Now that you have an idea about your destination, it's time to focus on positioning yourself in the marketplace.

In the "Position" chapter, you will:

- Learn where your skills and talents are needed by your current and maybe, future employer.
- Look at your résumé and make some quick updates to help you get noticed more frequently.
- Navigate LinkedIn differently so you can connect from a place of value and service as you intentionally build your network.
- Create a "Unique Professional Value Statement."
- Examine a job search and application strategy that will maximize your time and effort.

Many things can be found through Google, and because of that, there is no way this book can review such an exhaustively comprehensive list. Nevertheless, as a mid-career professional who hasn't looked for a job in some time, there is plenty of information to help you get started, take action, and build this portion of Your Mid-Career GPS to maximize your efforts and showcase your potential.

When Was the Last Time You Looked at Your Résumé?

One of the most significant components of building Your Mid-Career GPS is to have a résumé or CV (curriculum vitae – which is more often used by institutions of higher education and research professionals). So, where is it? You need to find your résumé, dust it off, and take an honest look at it to figure out how you will position yourself in this job market.

Once you find your résumé, make a copy of it and email it to yourself. This way, you know a copy of your résumé is appropriately filed somewhere in your email. Nothing can be more stressful than trying to figure out where the most recent copy of your résumé is located, especially since you probably have multiple versions of it anyway.

Your résumé is a living document designed to highlight and reflect your career experiences and value to a new organization. Résumés evolve. So one of the best things you can do at this point is free yourself from any judgment about its format or what it presently says about you.

There are three résumé formats. You will need to determine which one best reflects your experience and will be the best format for how you want to position yourself. The format most used is a chronological résumé. This format prioritizes your professional experience and accomplishments, beginning with your current position and working backward. In general, a chronological résumé will span 10 to 15 years.

A technical résumé will list your experiences, skills, employment history, and accomplishments about how you would succeed in a technical role. A technical résumé leads or highlights how your background matches explicitly or aligns with the job posting. Some like to refer to a technical résumé as a functional résumé. This kind of résumé can often be most helpful for people who have experienced an employment gap and are looking to return to the workforce.

The third type is a hybrid format. Here you're combining elements of a chronological résumé with a technical résumé. It's like you are taking the best components of both résumés into this format. Again, this format may be beneficial if you have experienced an employment gap.

As I review résumés, the most common mistake I see across all of my clients is that their résumé reads more like a job description instead of highlighting their specific accomplishments, achievements, and contributions. Your résumé needs to focus on the value you added or provided to your current and previous organizations. The best way to do this is to find specific data points or metrics to highlight where you have added the most value. You are looking for numbers, such as how much revenue you generated, how much money you saved by leading a project, or what percentage of time you saved by creating a new process. The more value you can highlight on your résumé, the more your résumé will strategically position you over your competition.

What is the Primary Purpose of Your Résumé?

Your résumé has one primary purpose, which is to get you an interview. In the job application process, we know that once the résumé clears the initial screening from the Applicant Tracking System and is seen by a hiring manager or human resources representative, they will decide whether to invite you to an interview.

Your résumé has one primary purpose, which is
to get you an interview.

A well-written résumé that is customized to the
job you are applying for has a far greater chance of
getting you an interview than merely sending out
your résumé over and over again. On my weekly
Facebook Live Show #84 – Why You Need a
Professionally Written Résumé, I interviewed
Porschia Parker-Griffin, the Founder and CEO of
Fly High Coaching. Porschia and I talked about the
importance of customizing your résumé and why
you must focus on how your résumé will get you
an interview. You can watch our conversation on
my YouTube Channel at
https://www.youtube.com/watch?v=rVKb3dgYRyA.

Why Does the Top Third of Your Résumé Matter?

According to Alyse Kalish in her article from The
Muse titled, "The 5 Big Things Recruiters Look at
on Your Résumé Before Making a Decision,"
recruiters will spend about six seconds on average
looking at your résumé before deciding whether to
continue reviewing it or moving on to the next

applicant. And while most recruiters will look at your work experience quickly, on the first pass, it's important to note that the top-third of your résumé matters. Our eyes gravitate toward the top of the page. In addition to including your professional contact information, including a customized LinkedIn URL, a well-written professional summary that highlights your areas of expertise is vital to getting you noticed more frequently.

Have a professional email address. I suggest a standard convention such as firstname.lastname@emailprovider. Make sure that your email provider is from one of the most current email providers. For example, a Yahoo or Gmail account looks far better than an email provider from the early 2000s that is no longer in existence. Plus, don't use your college student email address. You would be surprised how many I have seen! Lastly, stay away from "cute names" in your email address. If you apply for a leadership role at a company, they may not be fond of emailing you at "labradoodlelvr4189@emailprovider.com".

How Important is the Applicant Tracking System?

Think of the Applicant Tracking System (ATS) as artificial intelligence that will electronically compare your résumé to the company's job posting and give it a score. That score will determine whether someone reviews your résumé, and you may be potentially invited to an initial interview.

In an article for Jobscan, "Secrets of the Applicant Tracking System," Jon Shields describes "the Applicant Tracking System as a recruiting and hiring tool for companies that screen résumés based on a pre-determined set of criteria based on the job posting." Since the ATS is artificial intelligence, customizing your résumé to the job posting is essential. From the company's view, Shields mentions that it helps them manage a large influx of résumés and applications. Screening companies can sort and identify the candidates whose résumé most closely aligns with the job posting and move them to the top of the list. Then, those résumés will get screened by a recruiter, human resources professional, or hiring manager.

If you never clear the ATS, you will never get your résumé seen by a human being and be invited to that initial interview.

How Do You Customize Your Résumé to Make It ATS-Compatible?

It is essential to mention that while there is a science to writing a résumé, it is also very subjective. You could show your résumé to 10 different people, and more than likely, you will get 10 very different pieces of feedback. In some ways, the ATS makes it very clear that your résumé either matches what the company is looking for or it doesn't.

What you want to do when customizing your résumé to the job posting is to identify the key verbs and phrases in the job posting and insert them directly into your résumé. Make sure they are an exact match. For example, if the job posting requires client-facing experience leading a project and your résumé cites "customer service experience," that may not match.
Remember, we never want to lie on a résumé. However, if you can find synonymous experiences that pair directly with the job posting, it is in your best interest to use that specific language.

While chronological résumé formats tend to work best with an ATS, it's not to say that other formats wouldn't work. Remember to use a traditional font and standard résumé headings such as "Work Experience" and "Education." Trying to be innovative or creative with your titles or wording typically lessens your chances of clearing the ATS requirements.

Here are my top nine résumé tips. If you do these, you will accelerate your job search by having a résumé that works well for you and is getting you noticed.

1. **You need an excellent base résumé.**
   Think of your base résumé as a résumé that lists all of your experiences, accomplishments, and achievements. When you customize your résumé to the job posting, it is best to work from your base résumé. This way, you'll always have that one version of your résumé you can work from and easily customize when applying for positions.

2. **Customize your résumé to the job posting to give yourself the best chance of passing the initial screening with the ATS.**

    When I meet with clients, they often mention that they do not customize their résumés_to the job posting. This leaves them feeling frustrated and disappointed that their résumé isn't getting them invited to interviews. Yes, customizing your résumé to the job posting is hard work. But, if you want to give yourself the best chance of getting to an interview, then you need to go through that job posting, identify the key verbs and phrases, and make sure they appear in your résumé before you submit it.

3. **Choose a résumé format that best suits your situation.**

    Whether it be a chronological, technical, or hybrid format, make sure that the format you choose is most appropriate and best suits your current work and employment history. However, chronological résumés tend to perform best when being screened by the ATS.

4. **Focus on the top third of your résumé and make it stand out so when a human being reads it, it gets them interested in who you are and what you do.**

   You want someone looking at your résumé to get immediately interested in learning more about you and what you do. If your résumé is lackluster and doesn't highlight your skills, professional profile, and achievements accordingly, you will fall in with everyone else and never stand out and be recognized.

5. **Showcase where your skills are transferable to a new position.**

   Whether you are trying to make a career pivot or level up to a new position, make sure your skills are connected to that new position. In other words, you want someone to read your résumé, look at your experience and skills, and see where they align to the new role and how you will be an asset to their organization.

6. **Remember your résumé's purpose.**

   Your résumé's primary purpose is to get you invited to an interview. If you've read and reviewed your résumé and don't believe that it will help you move onto the next round, you need to go back and revise it. You want an interview because an organization is curious to learn more about what you do and how it will benefit them.

7. **Proofread your résumé and make sure it is free of all spelling and grammatical errors.**

   Not to take you back to your high school English classes, but you want to minimize any potential risks on your résumé. Yes, we are all human, and mistakes will happen. Nevertheless, if you can eliminate those mistakes, you're never going to give them something to question, whether it has to do with how detail-oriented you are or how much you proofread your work. You could invest in a program such as Grammarly, which I find is often better than the spell and grammar check in Microsoft Word. It is also a good idea to have someone else proofread it for you. Let's face it - it is your résumé, and you're a little close to it. That just means you won't often pick up on those minor mistakes because you've seen it too much. *(Side note: I can't tell you how many times my editor and I have reviewed this book. We hope there aren't any errors. However, if it happens, it's not because we did it intentionally. Sometimes, mistakes happen. We are human, and we just minimize risk as much as possible. When it comes to your* résumé, *don't beat yourself up if you notice a typo or error after it's submitted. Just fix it for the next time.)*

8. **Keep your résumé to two full pages in length.**

    As a mid-career professional, it is customary to have a two-page résumé. Make sure your résumé fills two full pages or gets to the one and three-quarter page mark. Typically, recent college graduates will have a one-page résumé. Senior executives may have a résumé longer than two pages.

9. **Get your résumé professionally written.**

    This will be one of the best investments you'll ever make in your career. If you are not an expert résumé writer, leave it to the professionals. They are more knowledgeable and better equipped to craft a résumé that will give you a much better chance of clearing the ATS than doing this on your own. For a few hundred dollars, you can save yourself a lot of time, energy, and frustration by having a professional write your résumé.

The Benefits of Having a Professionally Written Résumé

In 2009, I applied to several federal government positions and needed a particular résumé format to use with usajobs.gov. I spent hours agonizing over format and what to say, and how to align my experience to the job posting. And it was frustrating the hell out of me.

I talked to a friend who asked me why people hired me to tutor their children in mathematics. I replied that I was very good at what I did, and it alleviated some of the stress and tension the parents were feeling about teaching their kids, so they would just hire someone like me to help their children.

My friend looked at me and said, "Well, you are the expert. Right?" To which I replied, rather emphatically, "YES!"

She looked at me and said, "Stop being so damn cheap! Pay someone who is an expert to get your résumé professionally written and stop worrying about it."

And she was right.

I found an excellent résumé writer who was able to create a 15-page résumé for me. Now, thankfully federal résumés do not need to be that long. However, what I got was a phenomenal base résumé. While I never landed a position within the federal government, I created several customized versions of that résumé for the next three job positions I applied to. I got my money back in many ways from having my résumé professionally written.

If you can afford it, get your résumé professionally written. Find a service or résumé writer who is going to take time getting to know you and wants to see several job postings you are considering applying to, so they can write your résumé. Porschia Parker-Griffin and her résumé writing team are fantastic, and I have a lot of respect for what they do. Currently, I include a professionally written résumé in my private coaching package because my clients need it and they aren't expert résumé writers. Getting this done takes all of the stress and pressure from them having to write their résumé. And I always say, "Once you have a professionally written résumé, you can play."

You are investing in yourself and your career, and it will save you time, money, and stress. I've known people who, when asked what they want for their birthday or the holidays, have said "Money for their résumé fund." If it's important to you, you'll find the money. After all, how many lattes do you want to give up to get your résumé professionally written?

I've known people who, when asked what they want for their birthday or the holidays, have said "Money for their résumé fund."

One additional note – I do not write résumés. I promised myself when I launched my business full time that I would only do things I enjoy. (Thus, the joy of being a business owner.) And I don't like writing résumés. In the coaching relationship, I review résumés, but I am not an expert résumé writer. While I have learned many things about résumés over the years, I leave that work to the experts. That is why I partner with a résumé writer for all of my one-on-one coaching clients.

Do I Need to Submit a Cover Letter?

In Shelcy V. Joseph's article for Forbes (February 2020) titled "Do You Still Need to Write a Cover Letter?" she states, "Career site ResumeLab polled over 200 recruiters and HR pros to see if cover letters could tip the scales in candidates' favor. Below are some key highlights:

- 83% of HR professionals think cover letters are essential when making hiring decisions.
- More than 7 in 10 recruiters expect to receive a cover letter even if they are marked 'optional' in job ads.
- Less than 40% of applicants care to attach a cover letter even when it's mandatory.
- Over a third (36%) of hiring professionals start the evaluation process with the cover letter."

Unless the job posting explicitly mentions no cover letters or there isn't a place to upload one, I strongly suggest you write a cover letter with three key components.

In the first paragraph, introduce yourself. This is your chance to say why you are applying for the job and what interests you about the position. You've got a Unique Professional Value Statement. Use it! Get to the point and tell the hiring manager what you do and why you do it.

This needs to be in your first paragraph, along with information about how you heard about the position and your interest in applying for it. This is your chance to "be bold" and go after it. You've got just a few sentences. Don't leave anything in the bag. Put your reasons out there!

In the second paragraph, share your specific and relevant achievements and how your background and experience are perfect for this position. What have you accomplished that makes you an excellent fit for this job? Describe how your work aligns with the company's work and how your skill set addresses the employer's challenge addressed in the job posting.

Finally, in your last paragraph, have a strong call to action. Sometimes people need a little 'push," and your call to action is designed to help them decide. What do you want to ask in your call to action? Are you going to ask for an in-person interview? After all, a well-written cover letter and résumé are designed to get you to the next step in the interview process. Whatever your call to action is, make sure that it is specific enough for the hiring manager to know what you are asking. For example, avoid calls to action that aren't decisive, such as, "I appreciate your time, and I look forward to hearing from you." That's too vague, and honestly, it's not what you want. Consider something like, "Given my background and interest, I was wondering what availability you have over the next two weeks for us to have a preliminary call about my candidacy for this position?" Find the words that seem right for you, but make your call to action intentional.

Why You Need to Be on LinkedIn (Especially If You Don't Like Social Media)

LinkedIn is the number one professional site intended to help you network and connect with other like-minded professionals. While you may feel some kind of pressure to be on LinkedIn, it's understandable that many people find LinkedIn too overwhelming. Everyone has a different comfort level using social media. Maybe you enjoy

Facebook, Instagram, Twitter, TikTok, or being a part of the latest social media site. You may also be someone who despises social media. Let's acknowledge that some people use social media way better than you, and you are better than some beginners. Use LinkedIn for what you need and find your comfort level on how you choose to engage on the platform.

My friend and colleague, Rhonda Sher, known as "Your Connection Consultant," is an expert who helps professionals optimize their LinkedIn profiles and successfully navigate LinkedIn for their businesses and careers. Rhonda says, "If you're not on LinkedIn, you might be left out."

LinkedIn is a place where you get to connect with other professionals in your field and nationally recognized experts, search for jobs, professionally develop your skills, and build fantastic professional relationships.

Many of my clients express uncertainty or discomfort in how they use or don't use LinkedIn. Like any social media site, there is a learning curve. However, because LinkedIn is a professional site, and you are using this to network and expand your professional presence, I hope these tips will help you use LinkedIn a little differently than you have.

Why Does the Top Third of Your LinkedIn Profile Matter?

Much like the top third of your résumé matters, the top third of your LinkedIn profile matters as well. This will be the first thing someone sees when they visit your profile. They will take a few seconds to make an immediate decision as to whether or not they are interested in learning more about you and would like to connect. The top third of your profile contains your headshot, banner, and your headline. These have to stand out and represent your professional brand.

Make sure you have a great headshot. The photo that goes in the little circle inside of your banner needs to show your head, neck, and a little bit of your shoulders. This should not be a full-body photo. Use your smartphone, stand in front of a clean and simple background, and take your picture. Know that not having a headshot may indicate that you have something to hide or don't want to connect. I can appreciate and understand that some people are uncomfortable putting their image out on social media. However, LinkedIn is a professional site, and you are connecting with other like-minded professionals. According to Rhonda Sher, "You are 14 times more likely to have someone view your profile and 36 times more likely to have someone send you a message if you have a professional headshot."

The banner is valuable real estate that appears behind your headshot and can be customized. Once you have created your profile, LinkedIn uses a default banner. You can use a website such as Canva.com to create your customized LinkedIn banner for free. Use your banner to share something about yourself, such as a favorite quote, a statement about your professional values, or something that reflects your strengths. Your banner will help you reinforce your brand and if you have a website, be consistent with that as well. Pick two of your favorite colors and use them to create the background for your banner. Let your banner be a professional statement about what you do and who you are professionally. If you use LinkedIn for your business, use your banner to showcase what your business is about and share some contact information, such as your website.

Let your banner be a professional statement
about what you do
and who you are professionally.

Your headline, or what appears directly under your headshot, is a chance to communicate something specific about your professional self. Your headline can display your title. It can also express a statement, in the first person, about what you do and who you help specifically. LinkedIn gives you up to 220 characters to use here, which makes it valuable real estate and should include keywords so you can be more searchable.

For example, someone might have a headline that says, "Accountant at XYZ Company." You can change that to, "I help small businesses manage their finances and save money." You'll have "accountant" in your Work Experience section, but headlines are supposed to grab peoples' attention.

I had Rhonda Sher as my guest on my podcast #SHOWUP2020. You can listen to our conversation

- it's episode 16. Rhonda shares some excellent tips about these things, and I certainly encourage you to connect with her on LinkedIn. https://anchor.fm/showup2020/episodes/SHOW-UP-on-LinkedIn-ekkjra/a-a57pll

I can understand how LinkedIn can be a bit overwhelming, but there are some easy and quick things you can do to help you optimize your profile this week, or even in the next hour, to make you stand out more on LinkedIn. Think of this as a big stop sign on the highway where you want people to take a break from searching, stop at your LinkedIn profile, and get to know you a bit more.

1. **Update your headshot.**
   This is one of the easiest things to do. Find someone to take a photo of you with your smartphone, crop it, and upload it into your profile.

2. **Update your banner.**
   Visit Canva.com and create a customized banner. Take some time to look at other profiles on LinkedIn and see how they have used their banners. Find something that inspires you and reflects who you are. Remember that your banner is an

opportunity to make a personal, professional statement about who you are and what you do.

3. **Create a customized URL for your LinkedIn profile.**

   Use LinkedIn help or Google to get directions on how to create a customized URL for your LinkedIn profile. Also, make sure that your LinkedIn profile is hyperlinked on your résumé. This makes your LinkedIn profile more professional looking.

4. **Write a compelling About section.**

   When people look at your profile and decide to connect with you, they will read your About section, and the first three lines of your About section are the most important. You want to make sure you have enough in this section so the reader sees the words, "see more." This will get them to click on those words, expand your About section, and learn more about you. Rhonda Sher suggests including your contact information here and has a clear call to action at the end. Your call to action may be an invite to a virtual coffee or a brief 10-15 minute chat. You may also include a link to your website or a recently published article you want someone to read. Be creative here and find ways to keep people interested and engaged.

5. **Don't make your experience section read like a job description.**
Creating a profile that focuses more on the value you have added to your organization is far better than making your experience section read like a job description. Not many people are going to be enticed by reading about your job duties. They want to know more about your contributions and achievements. While it is acceptable to list some of your job duties, don't lose sight that LinkedIn is a great place to showcase your value and highlight your skills and expertise.

6. **Give endorsements.**
Endorsing your connections is a great way to build and maintain that professional relationship, while at the same time helping increase their LinkedIn SEO (Search Engine Optimization). Endorsements are very different than recommendations.

After I have connected with someone and had an initial conversation, I will thank them and endorse them in a few skills they shared with me during our conversation. Just like being a good networker, LinkedIn is all about giving. Make sure you are giving more than you are taking on LinkedIn. To endorse someone for a particular skill, click on the + next to that skill on their profile. Currently, a pop-up box will appear asking for some additional information about that endorsement. You can either fill that out or simply click on the X in the top right corner of that pop-up box to remove that pop-up. They will still get your endorsement.

If you don't have many endorsements, give some! This is the best way to increase your endorsements while helping someone grow theirs. Plus, it's always okay to ask for people to endorse you as well.

7. **Update your skills. (And pin your top three to the top of that section.)**
You can list dozens of skills in this section, but you can pin only three of those skills to the top of your section that everyone will see without having to click "See all." Make

sure that your most highly endorsed skills are the ones that are pinned to the top of this section.

8. **Recommendations make the difference.**
    If you are actively looking for a new position, I strongly advise that you have a minimum of five recommendations on your LinkedIn profile. This is important because recruiters and potential employers will read those recommendations. Long gone are the days when you would see "references furnished upon request" on your résumé. Today, recommendations can make a difference for you on your LinkedIn profile as you create your next advancement opportunity. Also, your recommendations must be reasonably current. After all, a recommendation from 10 years ago wouldn't showcase your current value.

    Visit someone's profile and scroll to the bottom. If you want to leave them a recommendation, click on the button that says, "Write a recommendation" or "Recommend <insert name>." That person must approve your recommendation before it appears on their profile. They may ask you to make a minor edit or change a few words just so the message is clear for everyone who reads it. This gives them complete control as to who can see what on their profile. Once they approve your recommendation, it now lives on their profile for everyone to see. (Quick Tip – If they don't have any recommendations, click the "More" button at the top of their profile under their banner and then click "Recommend" to submit your recommendation.)

Much like endorsements, I find the best way to get recommendations is to give them. When someone thanks you for giving them a recommendation, more than likely, they will return the favor. If they don't, it's more than appropriate to ask them to write a recommendation for you.

9. **Start making connections.**
Build your network intentionally. Connect with professionals who are doing the same work as you. Make connections with people who are doing similar work, but at a company you are interested in working.

Connect with people who are doing work you would like to do. It is best to include a short note explaining why you want to connect with that person and customize it, so they know you at least took a few moments to read their profile and get to know them a bit. First, it's less creepy. Second, and more importantly, you are very clear about your reasons and intentions for inviting them into your network and being a valuable resource. And remember, you are limited to 300 characters. I love what Rhonda says about connection requests. "Never just hit the Connect button. Always personalize your request."

Here's a simple, introductory message:

"Victoria,
I saw you work at <insert company> and as a <insert title>. I'm looking to connect with people in similar roles. You have an impressive profile.
I'd love to connect and be a valuable connection resource for you.
Sincerely,
John"

Here's another example where you ask a question to start a dialogue.

"Victoria,
I'm looking to connect with other <insert title> as I'm looking to move into that field.
What's one thing you enjoy about your job?
Thank you for answering my question, and I appreciate the opportunity to connect.
Sincerely,
John"

Once you've connected, now it is up to you to keep the conversation going. Building relationships, whether they be on LinkedIn or face-to-face, take time. Let the connection grow. Don't go from 0-60. Give them a chance to know, like, and trust you. One thing I enjoy doing is inviting people to a "virtual coffee" after a few exchanges. I find it's a nice break from typing and texting and setting aside 15 minutes to spend time getting to know someone. I also like using the voice message feature as well. It's different hearing someone's voice, and it's another great way to connect. Remember, being a good connection on LinkedIn is about giving. You'll be glad you did, and be a great connection on LinkedIn for hundreds, if not thousands, of people.

Should I Post My Résumé on My LinkedIn Profile?

If you want to post your professionally written résumé to your LinkedIn profile, you can upload the document and share it with your network. Viewers can download your résumé directly from your profile page. LinkedIn Help notes that you are not able to use that uploaded résumé for job applications. You will have to do that separately in the job application process.

You want to be mindful about directly copying and pasting your résumé into your LinkedIn profile in your "Experience" section. LinkedIn profiles are supposed to be more value-focused and expansive than your résumé. However, suppose you are actively job seeking and have an excellent base résumé. In that case, you could copy and paste those details into your LinkedIn profile, providing that base résumé highlights your key accomplishments and achievements for each position you've held.

Your LinkedIn profile is supposed to communicate your professional value, as evident by the work you've done and the achievements you've made. If your LinkedIn profile isn't showcasing your talents in that manner, you won't make the types of connections you desire.

How Do You "Play" on LinkedIn When You are NOT Looking for a Job?

There is nothing wrong with only using LinkedIn to help you network and find a job. For many professionals who are not active job seekers, it's understandable that they may take a break from LinkedIn or not access it as much as they had previously done. However, because of what we've seen due to COVID-19, virtually connecting was the *primary* way we stayed connected during lockdown and quarantine. And as things open up and we return to whatever the "new normal" will be, I firmly believe maintaining virtual connections is a new norm for us. This is why building your professional network on LinkedIn is critical for your success.

Like any group you belong to, you will determine your activity level based on how you want to engage and what you want to get out of it at any given time. Your work is pressure filled enough. You don't need to feel "guilty" about not being on LinkedIn enough. Let's just acknowledge that LinkedIn is there for you, for what you need, and when you need it. I like to think of LinkedIn where I can be "professionally fed and fulfilled" regarding everything from research articles, empowering discussions and posts, motivation, and relevant information to my field and work.

I like to think of being on LinkedIn as an opportunity to "play" and see who I can connect with and learn a few things. LinkedIn is *the* place to build your professional network. In 2020, I welcomed many opportunities to virtually connect with other coaches, business owners, career professionals, leaders, and other people who were interesting to me and invited them to a virtual coffee. And then, I connected with people who were curious to learn more about what I do as a career coach and how coaching could help them progress in their careers. Some of those people became clients.

Provide value through what you post and the comments you make on other's posts. This is a great way to engage and be seen on LinkedIn. I'm often asked what to post on LinkedIn, and I always respond that the best things to post are things you believe are valuable to your audience. If you found a great article related to your field, share the article and its link. Write why this article meant something to you. Ask a question you're curious about learning from your connections and see what they think about it as well.

Another great thing to post on LinkedIn is anything you find motivational or inspirational. If you use a graphic or image, make sure to give credit to the original author. Tag them in your post so they know you are sharing something of theirs. Motivational posts are massive on LinkedIn — especially in 2020. We can always use a little jolt or boost of inspiration when we are feeling a bit low. (If you want to see a great example of using motivational images to build your connections, connect with Rhonda Sher. She's an expert at it. Rhonda's URL is LinkedIn.com/in/RhondaLSher.)

If you have been approved to use LinkedIn Live, video is a great way to connect with your audience. Whether you go live by yourself or invite a guest to talk about a particular topic, video is a great way to build an instant connection. Not everyone feels comfortable being on video. We all feel like that in the beginning. If you like using video, it's a great way to share value and increase your visibility on the platform.

Lastly, remember that LinkedIn is a living document. You can update or change your profile anytime you want. Sometimes people feel the need to be "perfect" on LinkedIn. If we've learned anything from 2020, it's okay to be a little messy. We are all human. We have struggles. So when we share them, we build that "know, like, and trust" factor we crave when we want to connect. Ultimately, just be you on LinkedIn. People will like that. The more real you can be, the more you SHOW UP authentically and genuinely.

How Do I Know When to Accept Someone's Connection Request?

I get this question a lot. Understandably, you may be hesitant or fearful about connecting with people on this platform when you don't know them. You need to decide your comfort level when accepting requests from people you do not know.

Rhonda Sher shares some fantastic advice on this topic. She recommends that we only accept connection requests from people who we'd invite into our homes. I like this advice because it establishes a personal connection barometer.

If you get a connection request from someone and they have thousands of connections, and they look highly professional and reputable, then it might make sense to connect with them. However, after looking at someone's profile and seeing they only have a dozen connections and their profile isn't entirely written, and they don't have any endorsements or recommendations, you may choose not to connect with them. Also, think about building your network very intentionally. If someone reaches out to you and is doing similar work or working for a competitor, these may be valid reasons to accept their connection request.

Ultimately, you want to reach a milestone of 500 connections. Once you have more than 500 connections, your profile will only show 500+ in your headline. It's a significant milestone to achieve and lets people know that you have been active enough on LinkedIn to build a rather large following.

A Final Word About LinkedIn Versus Other Social Media Platforms.

LinkedIn is your professional marketplace. When I think of all the social media platforms--Facebook, Instagram, Twitter, TikTok, and others--it is recommended that you manage all your social media accordingly. Remember that your profile is public, and there are security and safety settings you can use to control how much someone sees your profile.

Someone told me years ago that if your grandmother would be appalled at what you were going to post on social media, then you probably shouldn't post it. Recruiters and potential employers can legally search your profiles to see what you have posted. Manage your social media accounts accordingly, and be aware of what you are putting out there.

Creating a "Unique Professional Value Statement."

A "Unique Professional Value Statement" (UPVS) is a sentence or two describing who you help and what you help them do specifically based on your talents and skills. Additionally, you can include a sentence about why this work is important to you. Some may refer to this as a "professional value proposition." The goal here is to create a statement that focuses on the value you bring to your work, your employer, and your clients.

A "Unique Professional Value Statement" (UPVS) is a sentence or two describing who you help and what you help them do specifically based on your talents and skills.

My UPVS is, "I help mid-career professionals change their career path in 90 days or less, without overwhelm, so they can prepare, position, and promote who they are and what they do, so they can SHOW UP to find a job they love or love the job they have."

What is the Difference Between a UPVS and a Pitch?

One of my favorite television shows is Shark Tank. I love seeing entrepreneurs come into the tank and pitch their products, hoping that one of the five amazing sharks will make an offer to invest in their product. To me, it is one of the best television shows out there. In just a few minutes, you decide whether you like the product, like the entrepreneur, and whether you root for them to get a deal.

People pitch on Shark Tank. To me, when you are networking or interviewing, it is in your best interest to communicate your value rather than pitch who you are and what you do. For me, a pitch can seem very "salesy." And when people pitch, they can seem very needy or desperate. No one wants to hire or connect with you if you are any of those things.

Indeed, there are times when a pitch may be more appropriate. For example, if you are at a networking event and are only given 10 to 15 seconds to communicate one quick sentence about who you are and what you do, then a pitch is certainly acceptable. But does your pitch honestly communicate your exceptional value to everyone in the room? Whenever you have an opportunity to share your unique professional value, take it. You will create more engagement, generate more genuine interest in who you are and what you do, and build a greater, more professional connection.

When Do I Use My UPVS?

When I help my clients create their UPVS, they are initially uneasy because it sounds awkward or different from what they are used to saying. However, once we've built their UPVS, they have a greater sense of excitement because they have a statement that encapsulates who they are and what they do. Then, they'll ask me when they get to use it, and my answer to them is, "Every chance you get."

You can use your UPVS at a networking event. You can share your UPVS when asked the dreaded "Tell me about yourself" question in an interview. You can practice sharing your UPVS in line at the coffee shop when you're having small talk with someone, and they turn to you and say, "What do you do?".

Practice saying your UPVS in your car. Stand in front of the mirror and practice saying it out loud. Turn on your smartphone and record yourself saying it. You must practice delivering your UPVS over and over again, so you can hear yourself saying it out loud.

This is a game -changer. By sharing your unique professional value, you are setting yourself apart from so many people who will play it safe and say something like, "I'm a teacher" or "I'm a project manager," or "I'm a <insert your job title>."

When we play it safe, we allow hearing us control the conversation based on their perception, impression, or experience about the job we said we do. When we change the dynamic and communicate our UPVS, we give them a little more information beyond our title. Now we get to share our value and let them decide whether or not they want to learn more about us.

How Do I Write My UPVS?

When I was building my business, my business coach Jeffrey St. Laurent walked me through a very similar exercise. This was going to be more than the headline that appeared on my website.

This would be how I would tell people that I wasn't just a "coach," but I was going to help them solve a specific problem. I took Jeff's model and expanded it to help my clients step into their unique professional value.

During my first meeting with a client, I ask them to tell me about themselves. This often results in a longer-than-needed explanation about all of the jobs they've held, where they've worked, and why they are feeling stuck. And when they finish, they often remark that their answer took far longer than they had intended. It's not only a great moment during our consult, but also a definite reflection on where they are at in their career journey and have lost sight of their vision and purpose for the work they are doing. They don't tell their story well, and they don't know how to communicate their value. It's as if, while they are telling their story, the tires are falling off their car, and they are left on this side of the road saying to themselves, "Well, that didn't go well."

To craft your UPVS, you must answer these three questions:

Who do you help?

What do you help them do specifically?

Why is this work important to you?

Let's take a look at some before and after examples.

Unique Professional Value Statement	
Before	**After**
"I'm an instructional coach."	"I help teachers improve their lessons through a coaching relationship, so they can improve their instructional practices and ultimately increase student achievement. I enjoy this work because it helps me reach more students and teachers to help everyone succeed."

Unique Professional Value Statement	
Before	**After**
"I'm an accountant, and I work with large firms that have over 5,000 employees."	"I help manage the financial accounting for larger firms with over 5,000 employees to help them not only manage their financial resources but also ensure the best allocations of those resources to new and current employees. I've always had a knack for organization and numbers. Today, I get to leverage that strength and help these companies."

Unique Professional Value Statement	
Before	**After**
"I'm a project manager for XYZ Company."	"I help manage a multi-million-dollar project for 'XYZ Company,' and I make sure that my team delivers that project on time and under budget. I like seeing my team come together and be super productive. After all, no one wants a project manager who comes in over budget and late!"

How Do I Know if the New Job is the Right "Fit"?

Part of your Mid-Career GPS includes positioning yourself based on how you have written your résumé, developed your LinkedIn profile, and created your UPVS. Now it is time for you to start looking at various positions. Whether you are looking to leave your current organization or seeking an internal promotion, you need to examine whether or not this new job is going to "fit."

This part of your journey can be a bit frustrating. You may feel as if you are sitting in traffic, only getting more and more frustrated waiting to hit the gas and get going. However, you've done a lot of work to get here, and sometimes, a slight pause in our journey gives us some time to reflect and think. That's why we can't overlook "fit" in our job search.

To assess "fit," you must look at the kind of work you will be doing, where you will work and the organizational culture, how much travel is involved, whether in daily commuting or overnight travel, who your clients will be, and how much you will be paid. Exploring "fit" is an opportunity to decide if the new job aligns with your attitudes, strengths, values, and talents. As you move through the application and interview process, you will learn more about whether or not this job seems right for you based on its "fit."

As you navigate this part of the career transition process, it's okay to look at "fit" from many different lenses. It's okay to explore. Maybe you need to take an exit or stop at the rest area and look around a bit. We do that when applying to multiple companies to see if we can find the right job. You have to do this so you can position yourself strategically.

Where Are the Best Places to Look for a New Job?

I like to say there are traditional routes for looking for a new job and some non traditional routes. For some, the most accessible place to look is online. Look at LinkedIn, Indeed, Glassdoor, Monster, and Google to search for jobs, as well as any other job posting sites online. For those seeking jobs within the federal government, usajobs.gov is your best source for looking at job postings. Many times employers will post their jobs on multiple sites to expand their applicant pool. Additionally, you may be able to visit the company's website. Under their Careers section, find what jobs are currently available and apply directly through that company's website.

While looking online may be the easiest or least intimidating for you, never underestimate the value of leveraging your network when looking for a job. GPSs are great, but sometimes you need to ask someone for directions. The same is true here. Suppose you have intentionally grown your network by inviting people who share similar professional backgrounds and interests as you. In that case, they may be a great resource to help point you in the right direction for finding a new job. They may be aware of an opening at their company. They may know someone who is actively looking for someone with the same skill set as you. You will never know unless you ask.

It may be difficult for some to leverage their network, be a little vulnerable, and ask for help. In 2020, we saw record unemployment, and it will take years for specific industries to recover due to this pandemic. Millions of people in quarter one of 2020 were projecting their best year. When the pandemic hit, their plans were shattered. It seemed almost overnight that people were laid off or furloughed. Some were fortunate to get severance packages, and others were not. Some may have felt disappointed and perhaps a little ashamed that this happened to them. For the first time in their career, they were uncertain about what was going to be next. While some had savings, many allocated that for retirement or something later in their lives and didn't want to touch it. Let's acknowledge that if you had savings or severance packages during this time, you were fortunate.

A career transition is a great time to assess how valuable your network is. Some may be able to help you. Others won't or are unable to. Letting people know that you are looking for employment is a great way to leverage your network. You never know when or how a connection is going to pay off for you. Think about reaching out to former colleagues, bosses, supervisors, HR representatives, friends, classmates, neighbors, and whoever may be able to give you a lead or a suggestion. Career transitions are messy, but they aren't something to be ashamed about either. It's one of the most common experiences we all share. We all change or transition our careers at some point. People know what it's like.

A career transition is a great time
to assess how valuable your network is.

These things take time. These conversations evolve. And while it may seem that looking online may produce immediate results for you, and that may be true, never underestimate or dismiss the value of your network and how they may SHOW UP for you. Who can you ask? Who can you contact that you haven't spoken to in a while? I bet they'll be glad to hear from you and might be able to help you.

Lastly, remember to return the favor whenever possible. I'm a firm believer in karma, and if you are a valuable connection resource for someone, then I believe it comes back to you.

How Often Should I Search for Jobs?

Every new client asks me this question. They come to their coaching session prepared to share an elaborate job search strategy they plan to implement or are currently implementing. Some say they will treat this as if this is their full-time job. They will share how they will work eight hours a day looking for jobs, networking, finding potential opportunities, and rigorously applying for new positions by customizing their résumés for each job posting.

While I celebrate and applaud them for these efforts, I am always curious to see how long their motivation lasts. Through my experience, I have noticed that, while this is a sincere effort, it quickly leads to my clients becoming exhausted, burned out, and frustrated by this entire process.

Honestly, while this is admirable, it is also completely unrealistic. Any job seeker is at the mercy of how many jobs are posted each week in their area of expertise. Yes, if you are currently unemployed and need to get back to work sooner than later, I believe you should adopt a mindset that finding a new job deserves your utmost attention.

There is a short game and a long game when finding a new position. Remember, you can apply every single day. But until that company pulls all the job applications and looks at all of the résumés, you may be waiting by your phone for weeks, if not months, before you are invited to that interview.

Here is what I recommend for my clients to help them with their job search strategy. Knowing that companies are posting jobs across multiple websites, know that you will repeatedly see that job posting. Dedicate two days each week to search for positions. For example, this could be Monday and Thursday or Tuesday and Friday.

Then, designate two other days a week to apply to those positions you found. Bookmark those job postings or create a tracker to chart your progress for applying to those positions. Here you will take the time to review the job posting and customize your résumé accordingly with those specific keywords and phrases you see listed.

Dedicate two days each week to search for positions. For example, this could be Monday and Thursday or Tuesday and Friday.
Then, designate two other days a week to apply to those positions you found.

Now that you have filled four out of your five days, use the fifth day as your Networking Day. For example, some of my clients like to designate Wednesday for this kind of work. On their Networking Days, they are actively reaching out and connecting on LinkedIn, scheduling virtual or in-person meetings (of course, during the pandemic, these were socially distanced meetings), joining local Meetup groups, or finding creative ways to network with people where they could become a valuable connection resource and vice versa.

If you are actively searching for a new job while you are currently working, there is no question this will take some time and a good balancing act. Adjust your schedule accordingly, but dedicate some time. Schedule it. Make it a priority one or two evenings a week or a few hours on the weekend to search and network. You know your schedule better than anyone. Protect your time to get this work done.

Like anything, you have to manage the stress. There is a wave of emotions that happens when you are actively searching for a job. Be aware of those emotions. Communicate when you feel incredibly frustrated, as well as overjoyed when you are invited to an interview or even a final interview.

My clients often share a sense of relief when I coach them through creating this specific job search strategy. Some have said it takes the pressure and the overwhelm away, knowing that they have the time to intentionally search for positions that precisely align with their skills, and apply accordingly. Creating Your Mid-Career GPS allows you to apply intentionally to positions based on where you will add the most significant value. This is a far better strategy than applying for every job you see and waiting to see if that spaghetti will stick to the wall.

Creating Your Mid-Career GPS allows you to apply intentionally to positions based on where you will add the most significant value.
This is a far better strategy than applying for every job you see and waiting to see if that spaghetti will stick to the wall.

Also, as you are leveraging your network, ask them if they would be willing to personally email or send your résumé to their boss or hiring manager. While you may still need to submit formally through their system, having a set of eyes on your résumé before it enters their ATS could be to your benefit.

How Do You Narrow Your Job Search or Home in on the Ideal Job?

Is there ever really an "ideal job"? I believe you can find a job right now. Sometimes people are looking for bridge jobs to get them from one awful situation into something better. Let's face it, our career paths are messy, and they are not perfect. As you are building Your Mid-Career GPS, the goal here is to find whatever is next. That's why you put all of that effort into the Prepare section we discussed earlier.

Think about the criteria this new job has to meet for you to apply. See where the new job aligns with your strengths and skill set. Get clear about what keywords will help you yield the best search results when looking online. You may even consider creating a pro and con list. On the "Pro" side, list all of the must-haves you want in a new position. Make sure these things are concrete and measurable. For example, a Pro might be "managing a team of 4-6 people." Don't use vague language in your Pro-Con list, such as "manage people." The more specific you are, the better your list will be. The same holds for creating your "Con" list. Take time to write out the things that are must-haves for you in this new position, as well as the things that you want to avoid as much as possible. We used a Pro/Con list in the Prepare section.

I have seen for myself, my clients, my friends, and my network that 2020 allowed us to figure out what we want in our careers and what we don't. I often say that 2020 was the year we got off the hamster wheel and looked inward about what we want in our careers, exploring what work-life balance looks like, and identifying where we get to make the most significant impact. Those are the things that need to go on your Pro/Con list.

Once you have created that list, look at your Pro side, and assign a point value to each item from 1 to 5. Get as clear as you can about the differences between a 5 versus a 4, a 4 versus a 3, and so on. Don't just assign the number 3 to everything on that side of your list. You need to prioritize those attributes. Then, do the same thing for the Con side. Once that is complete, add up the point values for each side and get a total. Which side has the greater total? That may give you an idea about whether or not the job is the right fit for you. Granted, this isn't scientific, but it does help. If you've never done this, I invite you to try it.

How Do I Know I Should Apply for a Job When I Don't Meet All of the Criteria in the Job Posting?

You are *never* going to meet 100% of the requirements for all the jobs you look at. I'm not saying that to crush your dreams. I'm saying that because it's the truth and, hopefully, makes you feel a bit better. It's just not going to happen. Companies create job postings with an extensive list of responsibilities and requirements to make their applicant pool as broad as possible. While this may be good for you, you still have to find ways to customize your résumé and stand out from your competition.

I coach my clients to look at a job posting and determine a percentage that reflects how well they meet all of the requirements for that position. That percentage is an arbitrary number. We create that percentage because it establishes a ground rule for them about applying for that job. For example, let's say you will apply to any position where you believe you meet at least 70% of the requirements. Once that happens, you commit to investing the time, effort, and energy to apply to that position. Keep track of where you applied and what percentage of those requirements you believe you met. Now, you will have some data as to whether or not your résumé cleared the ATS and you were invited to an initial interview. This data then gives you a confirmation as to whether or not your job search strategy is working for you or not. You can find a free tracker by visiting https://johnneral.com.

If you have time, I recommend leaving that percentage in place for a minimum of four weeks. By then, you should at least be getting some responses about your application status and whether or not that company wants to set up an initial interview. You can always change that percentage. We set such an allocation to stop you from applying to positions at random and desperately hoping someone will call you and invite you to an interview. Your Mid-Career GPS is a strategic and tactical process for helping you figure out what is next for you professionally. Set the parameters and stick to them so we can see if it works or not.

To continue building Your Mid-Career GPS, we covered these things directly related to strategically positioning yourself in the marketplace.

- Be clear about where your skills and talents are specifically needed. Focus on your

Unique Professional Value Statement and how you can help an organization.

- Customize your résumé when applying to each job posting to give you a better chance of meeting the criteria in that company's Applicant Tracking System.
- Update or optimize your LinkedIn profile so you can connect more intentionally with like-minded professionals and be a far better networking resource for them. Remember to send a note when connecting with someone and take time to build that network connection by keeping the conversation going, which may include a short virtual meeting.
- Take time to network and build connections with people who you appreciate and vice versa.
- Communicate your "Unique Professional Value Statement" wherever you can and to whoever is interested in hearing it. You are a valuable and talented employee. Use your talents to serve more fully.
- Create a job search and application strategy that will maximize your time and efforts.
- Give yourself a little space and grace to help you navigate this transition – whether

you are currently employed or not. Your Mid-Career GPS is a process. Give it time to work and manage your thoughts that your efforts are getting you one step closer to figuring out whatever is next for you professionally.

What is your Unique Professional Value Statement?

What do you need to do to get your résumé updated to where you feel confident submitting it for a job?

Based on the tips and suggestions provided, how do you plan to update your LinkedIn profile in the next week?

Outline a job search strategy based on your availability with your current schedule and your commitments. Make this something that is "doable" for you right now, whether actively looking for new jobs or spending time on your professional development.

Chapter 3

Promote – Let's Tell Everyone Where You Are Going

In the last two chapters, you've spent time preparing for your career transition and positioning yourself strategically in your organization or the job market. This work is vital to this next component of Your Mid-Career GPS. Now, it's time to promote who you are and what you do.

It's often challenging for my clients to talk about themselves in a way where they can promote who they are and what they do. My clients are heart-centered leaders. They easily put everyone else in front of them. They focus on the team rather than on themselves. So, when they are faced with a career transition or are preparing to interview, they will often sit back and rely on their accomplishments and achievements to speak for them, without advocating for why they are the best person for a particular position. I get it. This isn't easy, and it hasn't always been easy for me either. However, if you are going to get that next position or secure your next advancement opportunity, what you are about to learn here is vital to your success.

In this chapter, you will:
- Learn how to tell your story differently so you can get people *interested* in who you are and what you do, rather than merely finding you *interesting*.
- Increase your networking skills by focusing on your value and where you can be a great networking resource for someone.
- Identify ways you can navigate in-person and virtual networking events that feel authentic rather than feeling "fake."

- Create an interview preparation plan.
- Learn 10 things you must do in your next interview and 10 things you should avoid.

You Need to Be a Good Storyteller. After All, the Subject is *You*!

No one will tell your story better than you. We all have fans. These are our beloved colleagues and friends who eloquently champion our cause and share our story. But when we're at a networking event or interviewing for a new job, they aren't there with you. The spotlight is on you to tell your story.

Social media has dramatically affected how we tell our stories and have limited the time we have to make a good impression. Just like the initial view of your résumé and LinkedIn profile, you only have a few seconds to make that first impression. Learn to tell your story well and get them *interested* in who you are and what you do.

In an article for Fast Company called "Want To Be A Great Storyteller? First, Break These Habits" by Anett Grant, Grant shares some practical and valuable tips to help you tell your story, such as, don't give too much background. Remember, when you are telling a story, you need to provide people with enough context. One of the biggest mistakes people make when networking and interviewing is that they talk too much. Give people just enough information to understand and relate to what you were talking about and follow the general rule that if you feel like you are talking too much, then you are.

Lastly, Grant advises not to "take your audience through unnecessary detours." While the embellishments and enhancements may be interesting to us, they can often take our audience away from our story's intent. I think this is one of the many reasons why TED Talks have become so popular. Share your story in a limited amount of time to leave people wanting more, their curiosity peaked, and feeling better for having invested their time listening to you.

I can attribute my ability to being a good storyteller from my years as a middle school mathematics teacher. I have often joked that if you want helpful feedback about how well you are doing, become a middle school teacher because those students will give you honest and sometimes brutal feedback. A good storyteller can take the audience's pulse, manage it, and leverage it to keep the audience in the palm of their hands. It's another reason why great comedians do a fantastic job of pulling their audience along by sharing their stories and getting them to laugh.

Get Someone *Interested* in Your Story Rather Than Finding You *Interesting*.

We are all interesting human beings with fantastic stories about what we have done and where we have been. But there is a vast difference between someone finding you interesting and someone being interested in you.

When someone is interested in you, their questions are different. Their level of engagement has shifted energetically because they are curious to learn more about you. Numerous studies about nonverbal communication cite when someone leans in or toward someone, it is a sign they are fully engrossed in the conversation, wanting to learn more.

When someone is interested in you, their questions are different.

For career professionals who struggle at networking events or interviews, getting someone interested in your story is critical to building that relationship. You must figure out what will catch their attention. Be energetic. Tell your story as if you not only believe what you are saying, but also you are passionate about it. Energy is infectious. Avoid being the quintessential "Debbie Downer" who does nothing but drain your energy and suck the life out of you. To me, there is nothing worse when this happens at a networking event or during an interview.

Consequently, the opposite can happen. When you have a conversation with someone whose energy is up, positive, motivating, and inspiring, you are attracted to that. You want more of what they have and are interested in learning more.

Reflect on how well you tell your story. Examine the kind of engagement and environment you create with colleagues, whether it be in a team meeting, over a cup of coffee, or sitting in a virtual meeting. It's in your best interest to be a better storyteller.

Making Your Mess Your Message

My day begins every morning at 7:00 am, watching Good Morning America. I am a Robin Roberts fan. When Robin was diagnosed with breast cancer in 2007, and then five years later diagnosed with a rare form of cancer, she opened up about her diagnoses on air. Whether you are a fan of hers or not, you could feel her pain, worry, deep faith, and support of her loved ones and dear friends as she navigated these uncharted waters.

One of the strongest forces in Robin's life was her mother. Robin tells a story about how her mother encouraged her to not only embrace her diagnosis but also to share it by reminding her that her mess is her message. She reminded Robin that she had a platform many people don't have. She had a secure job, great benefits, wonderful people around her, and a diagnosis that was rare and frightening. But her mother reminded her that by sharing her story and making her mess her message, she was going to reach millions of people, inspire them, move them, and help them take action because of what she was experiencing.

We all have a mess. In my book, "SHOW UP – Six Strategies to Lead a More Energetic and Impactful

Career," I shared how my mess became my message. I shared an event that happened to me when I was 10 years old that dramatically shaped the path of my life to where it is today. While those events were not easy, I am grateful for them. Those events help me tell my story.

You have a story and a message. You don't need to be a published author, a well-known news personality, or a celebrity to share your story. You can do this just as easily with one of your dearest friends or trusted colleagues. You control the message. You decide what it is you want to share when you tell your story. Just know that your story is powerful, and someone is ready to listen to it.

The Totality of Your Experiences Have Brought You to This Moment

In late 2012, I found myself interviewing for a position I believed I had no right interviewing for but was willing to go through the process. A former boss had advised me to interview and thought the job would be a great fit and opportunity to level up.

I did all of the things I'm sharing with you. I customized my résumé. I wrote an excellent cover letter. And like you, I waited. I initially had a phone call with an HR representative and was invited to a half-day interview. The interview would begin with me taking an assessment and then meeting with various people inside the organization, including the executive vice president and a handful of other senior leaders and decision-makers.

I arrived for my interview well before my scheduled time. I was nervous and excited and a little uncertain about how well this job would be an excellent fit for me. I took that assessment and felt as if I bombed it. While I certainly had the technical skills, I knew I would be trained to learn their processes as well. But there were some things based on the difficulty of the questions or the time constraint I had been given that I just didn't feel confident about how well I had done. We all can get into our heads and let our inner critics take over, especially during an interview.

Next, I met with the executive vice president. Admittedly I don't get overly nervous in interviews, as I have interviewed plenty of times in my career. I like to think of interviews as a "get to know me" opportunity. Overall, this was a good conversation, but I didn't leave their office feeling exceptionally confident, especially after believing I had bombed the assessment.

I met with more people and was often asked the same questions. I maintained consistency, delivering the same value-added response and communicating my UPVS as much as possible. However, something didn't feel right. Mindset is everything. If you believe you've bombed in an interview, your energy shows.

Next, I went to interview with one of the directors. As I walked into her office wondering how much longer the day would be, I decided I had nothing to lose. I set a ground rule to approach this interview, focusing on the next conversation and not focusing on the outcome. I was not going to hold myself back in any way. I would release myself from any judgment and just be the best John I could be in this interview.

Remember, I'm thinking there is no way they were going to offer me the job. At one point, she looked at me and asked, "Why should we hire you?" I decided to go for the joke. I shared that "I had spent 14 years at a wonderful district in Northern New Jersey. I then came to Washington D.C. and had spent 14 months working for the District of

Columbia Public Schools. I then went to work at the State Superintendent's office and had spent 14 months there." I looked at her and said, "I'd like to make it to 15 somewhere. Do you want to give me a job?"

She looked at me somewhat puzzled and a little perplexed at my silliness in answering her question. After an awkward chuckle from both of us, I leaned in and said, "All joking aside, here's why you hire me. You hire me because I'm good with people. And while I have certain technical and content expertise and believe that on some level, I probably bombed the assessment, my technical knowledge is good, and you can train me to get that technical expertise to the level where you need it. But where I am most valuable is that I know how to build relationships. I know how to build teams. And if you have teams that aren't functioning as well as possible, then I'm good at repairing dysfunctional teams. I am also really good with clients. So if you need someone like me with my skill set, that's why you hire me for this job."

There, I said it. I didn't hold back. I told my story from a place of value and service. And I knew that if she were looking for someone like me, I'd be offered the job. I left the interview, knowing I did the best I could. A week later, I was offered the job and accepted.

I was on the job for about three months when that same director walked into my office late one afternoon and closed my door. I'm not going to lie to you. I thought I was getting fired. We all have that inner critic in our heads telling us why we aren't good enough. I figured this was it. I'm getting fired. She knew me well enough to begin the conversation by saying I was doing good work, and she was glad I was there. By the end of that conversation, she had invited me to accept a new position. This position would work directly alongside her and help her manage our 25+-member team's day-to-day operations. During that conversation, she told me she hired me for this position. Over the next five years, I navigated through two re-organizations, had roles specifically created for me and my areas of expertise, and enjoyed working with a great group of people and amazing clients.

So you may be wondering why I left. I created my next advancement opportunity because I had realized that what I wanted to do was not possible in this organization. While met on some level, my love for coaching and professional development would not be fulfilled in bringing and creating an internal coaching program to that organization. The organization was experiencing tremendous growth. There was a business decision to move the organization in a particular direction, where they needed me to focus more specifically on onboarding and training. I wanted to coach, and it didn't look possible for me to do it there. Plus, I had that moment where I questioned whether or not I could stay in this position until I was ready to retire. And my answer was, "no."

I was and still am crystal clear on the value I provide every day. It allows me to tell my story and where I get to help my clients the most. Without question, this is the best work I have ever done in my career. I have loved every job I have held, but I love this one the most because it is where I get to have my most significant impact. I am here because of the totality of my experiences. Everything I have done, every place where I have worked, and every person I have worked alongside and managed or led has brought me to this point.

My wish for you is that as you continue to build Your Mid-Career GPS, you find the best way to position yourself from your greatest value and ability to serve wherever you work. Tell your story from a place of value and service as much as possible. It will lead to the most incredible professional happiness you've ever had.

What Holds You Back from Telling Your Story?

There are many reasons why people shy away from or hold back on telling their story. Some are fearful about how their story will be received or judged. Their inner critic gets the best of them and holds them hostage, from sharing their value and experiences. This is one of the many reasons why coaching can be a powerful professional investment in your career. When you know your value and communicate it authentically and unapologetically, you SHOW UP very differently.

Who loses out when you don't share your story from a place of value and service? When you believe you have something of incredible importance to offer to an organization or someone you work with, why wouldn't you tell your story? When you hold yourself back from telling your story, you are willing to silence your voice because you don't believe what you have to offer will help someone. Is that what you want? Does the world need you to be silent?

How Do I Help Someone Tell Their Story?

First, I have all of my clients identify five powerful stories that are monumental in their careers. A story could be about a particular accomplishment, achievement, or recognition. It might be a pivotal moment that dramatically changed their career. Make a list of your five stories. Write down enough to remember about what happened in that event.

Next, take one of those stories and imagine putting all of the details and background information from that story into a bucket. Fill your bucket with as many details as you can about that story. All stories need a clearly defined beginning, middle, and end that take the listener on a journey that paints a vivid picture of what your story means to you.

Development Dimensions International, or DDI, created the STAR (Situation or Task, Action, Result) method to answer any behavioral interview question. These are the questions that typically begin with, "Tell me about a time," "Share an example when," "Describe a time when you," or "Explain how you." This universally recognized protocol for crafting your response focuses on the Situation or Task, the Action you took to address the situation, and the Result, which describes how your actions were measured and effective. If you struggle to answer these behavioral questions, I strongly encourage you to use the STAR method because it will help you structure your response with a clear beginning, middle, and end that focuses on your role and your results based on your efforts.

I will share more with you about interviewing in an upcoming section. For now, it is crucial to know as many details about your five stories. They are your stories. Thus, you need to tell them better than anyone else. Know the benefits of each story. Focus on what you achieved or the results you created in that story. Talk about what you learned or how you improved. Be clear about the message you want to convey.

I invite you to watch several people you consider to be great storytellers to listen and watch how they deliver their message. While there are many fantastic speakers on YouTube and other social media sites, people are chosen to give a TED Talk because they are excellent storytellers with a powerful message. A great storyteller pulls you closer and creates a powerful connection. You are interested in what they have to share and are hungry to hear more of their life, experiences, and stories.

A great storyteller pulls you closer
and creates a powerful connection.
You are interested in what they have to share and
are hungry to hear more of their
life, experiences, and stories.

Your story must always have an obvious beginning, middle, and end. Your story needs to grab the reader or listener's attention and hold it. When that happens, your audience is connected in some way to your story and is interested in learning more. That is how you tell a great story. You have to practice. You have to study. You have to deliver or communicate your story multiple times – perhaps hundreds or thousands of times – before you get good at it.

When you become a great storyteller, you are promoting who you are and what you do from that place of value and service, as we discussed earlier. And trust me, people will be interested in hearing more from you. You have a lot to offer. Promote yourself and what you do.

What is the Purpose of Networking?

In 2020, we saw in-person networking events come to a screeching halt because of the pandemic. Let's face it. Virtual networking events do not have the same energy or productivity as in-person networking events have. Nevertheless, the purpose of networking, whether virtual or in person, is to build meaningful business relationships. Your goal in any networking event is to serve first and be a valuable networking resource for someone before asking for whatever you want or need.

A good networker is someone who puts themselves second. While years ago, people would venture to networking events and immediately ask for a sale, a referral, or even a job, things have thankfully changed over the years. Networking has become more about service and connection than it has about immediately going for the ask. There is nothing wrong with asking for what you need, but it has to come at the right time and place. Networking is about finding opportunities to make a connection with someone.

A simple question, such as, "How can I help you?" will serve you far better in a networking conversation than leading with whatever you want, such as a new job or an introduction. When I coach clients on the benefits of networking, it's understandable that they will immediately jump to how that person can connect them or help them find a job. This can come across as being "a little needy" and potentially be a huge turnoff. Remember, networking is about building relationships—first impressions matter. Be someone willing to serve and connect. Give first and get later. When it comes time for you to ask for what you want, it will be much easier for you and far better received.

A simple question, such as, "How can I help you?" will serve you far better in a networking conversation than leading with whatever you want, such as a new job or an introduction.

Get Networking Right.

You're meeting someone new, or you've been introduced to someone who's a mutual connection. Slow down. Ask questions. Get curious about what they do and see if there is a way you can help them. If you immediately focus on the outcome – such as will they hire you, give you an interview, or connect to someone, without them getting to know you a bit first, you are missing a huge opportunity. Plus you'll come across as being super needy. Don't be so forceful. Like any good relationship, it takes time to build. Let things progress naturally and evolve.

No one wants to connect with someone who communicates urgency or desperation. People will run away from it. Networking is like professionally dating someone. You need time to determine if this is a relationship worth having. Just like dating, I don't believe any networking relationship is always 50-50. By this, I mean that there will be times you will find yourself giving more than you are receiving. And that is okay. This is not about balancing everything out so things are equal. Strive to give more than you receive. When you serve more than you take, you will find yourself getting more than you ever imagined. Find ways you can help them. Are they looking for resources or introductions? Do they need connections or referrals? Anything is possible. It's your job as a good networking connection to listen to what they need and determine if you can help them.

I have several networking connections who have become wonderful referral partners. There are times when I am referring more people to them and their businesses than they are to me, and that's completely fine. Because I know that down the road, the tide will switch. When you focus on what's in it for me, you lose sight of the purpose behind networking. Serve fully and ask later. You'll know when it's time to ask for what you need. And if you've been a good networking connection and helped them, they'll ask you.

The biggest and most fatal flaw you can make when networking is to make it all about you. Do this at one networking event and you'll be forgiven. Do this at multiple networking events and you will earn a reputation, causing people to avoid you at subsequent events because they don't want you in their network. You'll know when this happens because they will run or they always "have to go to the bathroom."

How Do You Navigate an In-Person Networking Event?

As we begin to open up and return to what "normal" used to look like pre-pandemic, good, old-fashioned networking events will return. For some, this will be another stressor they would choose not to face.

In-person networking events can be stressful. Many people are uncertain how to navigate the room, begin a conversation, and wonder if they are playing by all of the rules to be a good networker. Remember, a good networker is someone who builds meaningful business relationships by serving first and asking later.

In her Forbes article, "17 Tips to Survive Your Next Networking Event," Darrah Brustein recommends you don't spread yourself too thin. Given how overwhelming networking events can be, it is essential to have a strategic plan going into the event. When I'm working with my coaching clients, I coach them on setting a ground rule for making a certain number of connections at that event. Sometimes this number is one. To make a networking event successful, all you need is one great connection. Granted, some people try to get the most out of the event that they can. And I applaud them for that. You know yourself best and what you can and are willing to tolerate. Pushing yourself is one thing. Stressing yourself out is something else. I usually believe that if I can make one to three great business connections at an event, it's a success. And I always follow up with them after to see how we can continue the conversation.

When navigating a networking event, Brustein recommends having a few great questions to ask to help get the conversation started. I particularly like her article because she recommends treating these networking events like a puzzle. Remember, you are a connector. Think about the people in your network who would be a valuable connection resource for someone you are meeting. She says that if everyone had that outlook, these events wouldn't be as stressful. Again, networking is all about how you can serve, support, connect, and help others.

Lastly, I believe it's always a good idea to bring someone along with you to an in-person networking event. This way, it's an excellent opportunity for you to divide and conquer, share and compare notes, and go out for dinner or a drink afterward so you can both decompress and process how the event was for you both.

How Do You Navigate a Virtual Networking Event?

2020 was the year of the virtual meeting. I have attended several virtual networking events, and while some of them were good, some of them were particularly awkward and left me wondering whether or not this was the best use of my time.

An excellent virtual networking event needs a great host. This person knows how to manage a virtual event and is well versed in managing the technology to keep things moving. In his article, "10 Tips for the Best Darn Pandemic-driven Virtual Networking," Frank J. Kenny suggests that you prepare for this event just like you would an in-person networking event. He recommends that you remember acceptable networking practices and have a specific goal for what you want to get out of the event. Having a clear plan will help you SHOW UP authentically and genuinely for navigating that event.

Additionally, Kenny recommends you bring a positive attitude and avoid the negative. He says, "it's easy for a virtual networking event to turn into a giant convention of Eeyores." Keep the complaining and the negativity to a minimum and find a way to navigate that event, make some connections, do some follow-up, and build your professional network with people you want to have in it.

I like virtual networking events. First, there is no travel, and sometimes it can be pretty difficult hearing someone in a crowded, noisy room. And given what's happened in 2020, I don't see virtual networking events going away. Whether your preference is in person or virtual, know that networking is an integral part of Your Mid-Career GPS. If you're not good at networking, that's okay. But remember that this needs to be a part of it. The more practice you get, the better you will be.

How Many Virtual Coffees Can You Have?

I happen to like meeting someone for a virtual coffee. They are simple. These are one-on-one meetings with someone I'm trying to learn more about and get to know. And in 2020, I had a lot of them – far more than I had in 2019. And I plan on having more of them in years to come.

Granted, hosting a virtual coffee puts more responsibility on you, especially when you have invited someone. You want to make sure you have a clear agenda and goal for the meeting. In her article, "Five Tips for a Successful Virtual Coffee Catch-Up," Natasha Buddy interviewed KPMG Partner Stef Bradley. She has some excellent tips in this article. Still, the ones that resonated the most for me were planning your meeting, minimizing any distractions that will take away from you building that connection with your guest, and keeping it short and slow. Promoting who you are and what you do comes across in many ways. Inviting someone to a virtual coffee and then making them feel as if they are being rushed through this conversation to get to some goal may leave them feeling frustrated and disappointed. Make the time enjoyable. You are meeting someone new and getting to know them. Just as we've discussed before, let the conversation evolve and see where it will take you. And as always, remember to serve first and ask later.

Why is Networking Like Building a Circle of Friends?

Because networking is an integral part of building Your Mid-Career GPS, find a way to network that is comfortable for you. The goal here is to create a network of like-minded professional connections you can support and vice versa. Like any relationship, it takes time to evolve and get it to where you can know, like, and trust someone. This means you may have more than one meeting or virtual coffee with someone before things start to happen.

Because networking is an integral part of building Your Mid-Career GPS, find a way to network that is comfortable for you.

When I'm networking, I often ask, "How can I be a valuable networking connection for you?" In general, their response is priceless. I'll hear things like, "I don't know how to answer that because I've never been asked that before." or "What a great question! Let me think about that."

Reach out to like-minded people and grow your network intentionally. Connect with people who you would be honored to have in your network. Build your networking circle with quality people you can support, and ultimately they will help you as well.

Strengthening your networking muscles takes time and repetition. Make the time and a concerted effort to practice your networking skills and build those relationships. In 2020, we learned that we could develop valuable connections with people, even when there is a screen between us. People will sense your energy and your willingness to connect. Let networking be a valuable part of Your Mid-Career GPS and find a way to make it happen.

Sharing a Few Personal Networking Tips

I've networked enough that I know what works for me and helps me grow my business. However, I've learned a few things along the way that I want to share with you. So, let's get real for a minute.

You may encounter someone who is very clingy and needy. Every time you try to politely leave, they find a way to pull you back in. One time, I had someone waiting for me outside the bathroom after I politely excused myself. (Yes, that was creepy.) If something like this happens to you, you need an exit strategy. That's why bringing someone with you to an in-person event can be helpful. You'll need some signals or codes, plus it makes the event more fun for you both. Find the words to politely excuse yourself and let the person know the conversation is over for now. You may say something like, "It's been great talking to you, and I can't believe how quickly the time has flown. I promised myself I would make a few connections at this meeting, and I want to talk to a few more people. Let's exchange contact information, and we can follow up after the event." Now, if you don't feel comfortable exchanging contact information, don't. And if they continue to try and monopolize your time, politely remind them of your intention to meet more people and leave.

Ask around for what the best networking events are in your town or community. Word of mouth will spread when someone has a great networking event or a bad one. See if someone can invite you as their guest to the next event. Leverage your existing network to help you grow your connections.

When you follow up with a new connection after the networking event, take some time to debrief and inquire about how the network event was for them. Ask them what they learned, who they were surprised to meet, who was a great connection, and how they usually follow up with people. You may get some new ideas on how to navigate your next event. I have one valuable connection I always debrief with after a networking event when we attend together. It's an excellent opportunity for us to compare notes and help each other connect as well.

Find opportunities each week to network with someone individually. This could be someone who's already in your network but someone you haven't spoken to in a while, or it's a new connection. According to a CNBC article by Julia Freeland Fisher titled, "How to Get a Job Often Comes Down to One Elite Personal Asset, and Many People Still Don't Realize It," Fisher found that "70% of all jobs are not published publicly on job sites and as much as 80% of jobs are filled through personal and professional connections." This is why networking is vital to your career success and why it must be an essential part of promoting who you are and what you do. Build your network intentionally with great people you want in your circle and people you know who you can help and then can help you when needed.

You've Got the Interview! Now What?

I have interviewed hundreds of people and have screened thousands of résumés throughout my career. As much as I have loved being the candidate during an interview, I have also enjoyed my time being on the other side of the desk. I appreciate and respect when candidates are nervous. They're just being human and letting me know how deeply they care about putting their best foot forward and want the position. Interviewing is a skill and an art. How you SHOW UP for an interview, much like how you SHOW UP for your life and career, matters.

I coach my clients that there are two main reasons for interviewing. First, it is to build a relationship with the hiring manager and other interviewers. Secondly, it is to get the hiring manager *interested* in who you are and what you do. Take note that I never said the purpose of interviewing was to get the job.

One of the biggest mistakes people make when interviewing is they get completely hyper-focused on the outcome, as in, being offered the position. All this does is pull your attention and energy from SHOWing UP authentically and genuinely in this conversation. An interview is your chance to showcase your value and how you can serve in this new organization by using your skill set to solve the problems they have listed in their job posting.

One of the biggest mistakes people make when interviewing is they get completely hyper-focused on the outcome, as in, being offered the position.

I get it. You want the job. You want the opportunity and the compensation that comes with it. But if that is the primary thing you are focusing on, you will never be present in the conversation and won't build the relationship you need and make the impression you want.

10 Things You Must Do in a Job Interview

To help you build those relationships and get the hiring manager and interviewers interested in who you are and what you do, here is my list of 10 things you must do in a job interview. These things will serve you well whether or not you are interviewing in person or virtually.

1. **Answer the "Tell me about yourself" question better than your competition.**
   This is the perfect time for you to communicate your UPVS. Avoid doing the "Experience Walk" or regurgitating what is on your résumé. It is insulting to the hiring manager and the other interviewers because you make it seem like they didn't read your résumé. They want to know you beyond what you have on your résumé or your LinkedIn profile. This is an excellent opportunity to be memorable and begin building that relationship. Get them interested in who you are and what you do. Also, if you are comfortable doing so, find something personal and appropriate to share with the hiring manager and the interviewing team. For example, I always ended my response to this question by sharing my love for game shows and that I am a professional bowler. If anything, I could pretty much guarantee that no one who interviewed for this job along with me loved game shows and was a professional bowler. At least I was memorable.

2. Be clear on why you want the job.

Be honest about why you are applying for this job. It is perfectly acceptable to share that you have learned there is no more room for you to grow at your present company, or the advancement opportunity you would like to have there is not going to happen. There are ways you can communicate why you want the job and what caused you to apply without being negative or throwing your company under the bus. Because of the pandemic and more people being unemployed than ever, it is acceptable to simply let a potential employer know that you were furloughed or laid off due to the pandemic, and you are actively seeking new employment. If there has been a substantial gap in time from when you were last employed, make sure you find an opportunity to share what you have done to enhance your professional development during that time. Potential employers want to know what you did with your time during the pandemic and what you learned.

3. **Do your research on the company.**

   Make sure you know what the company does and who it helps, along with its mission and vision. This will help you structure any questions you want to ask at the end of the interview. Make sure you know what the company stands for and what its brand represents. You never want to be caught off guard when asked what they do, and you can't formulate a coherent answer. Lastly, as you read reviews online, treat any review like you would a Yelp review. There is probably some truth, perhaps a little embellishment, and it is up to you to ultimately decide when offered the position if that is where you want to work.

   Additionally, know what kind of interview you will be having. It is acceptable to ask the recruiter or HR representative if the interview will be primarily technical, mostly behavioral, or a hybrid of both. This will help you prepare for the interview and reduce any unnecessary stress.

4. **Lock down the logistics.**

   This can be easily overlooked and cause you a lot of stress leading up to the interview. If you are meeting in person, make sure you know where to go. Have clear directions and give yourself plenty of time to get to the site. If you are meeting virtually, make sure all of the technology works ahead of time. For example, if you feel very comfortable meeting by Zoom but learned that the meeting would be on Microsoft Teams, make sure you have downloaded all of the necessary software and tested it out for your interview. It never looks good if you show up late to an in-person interview. It looks even worse if you are late for a virtual interview or you can't get the technology to work correctly.

5. **Find a way to manage your virtual space.**

   When attending a virtual interview, make sure your background is professional, free of clutter, and represents you as professionally as possible. The internet has been cruel to judge peoples' backdrops when interviewed on television. I'll never forget the comments people made about how much of a mess Dr. Fauci's office was during interviews about the COVID-19. Having an unprofessional background can be very distracting.

Make sure your camera works and delivers a clear picture—the same thing for your microphone. While most smartphones and current laptops have excellent cameras and microphones, make sure to test them as well. Additionally, my best friend from high school and professional videographer, Robert Rinkewich, owner of Vision Photo and Video, LLC, recommends that you position the camera, so your eyes are in the top-third of your screen. This will frame you accordingly on video and ensure a strong visual presence for you.

Additionally Robert suggests that you make sure you can be heard clearly. Many people rely on the built-in microphone on their devices. While some work well, others may make you sound as if you are muddled or pick up a lot of background noise. The last thing you want is for someone to not hear you clearly. Consider purchasing an external microphone that is wired and directly connected to your computer. Sometimes, wireless or Bluetooth mics can add a delay to the audio. Whether it's a virtual work meeting or interview, it's imperative you can be seen and heard clearly.

Also, make sure your lighting is appropriate for your space. When you are in a virtual meeting, people want to see you. There are many affordable and very good options when it comes to lighting kits for your home office or virtual space. Having poor lighting only makes you look bad – literally and figuratively.

Lastly, make sure your device is fully charged and plugged into an outlet. It never looks good if your battery runs out in the middle of an interview.

6. **Be great at the STAR method when answering behavioral interview questions.**
   I shared earlier about the benefits of using DDI's STAR method. Make sure you practice how to frame your answer using this protocol. Additionally, strive to keep all initial answers under two minutes. This

will give you a break from talking and allow the hiring manager or other interviewers to ask follow-up questions based on your response. Also, make sure to highlight the results in your STAR method response. Candidates often overlook the results they've created because they are focusing too much on the details.

7. **Be mindful about what you say, how you say it, and how long it takes you to say it.** How we SHOW UP energetically and how well we communicate are key factors in an interview. Be careful of using filler words such as "um," "like," "so," "you know," and "ahhh." Let's also acknowledge that when used sparingly, they can provide for a moment to pause and think about your response. Using too many filler words can be very distracting. Speak competently and confidently. There is no need to be cocky. Let your personality shine through.

Watch your verbiage when answering specific questions. For example, when you are asked a question about your opinion, it is acceptable to begin by saying, "I think." However, when you are asked a question that draws on a particular experience or background you've had, beginning your response with "I think" may cause the hiring manager or interviewer to question your confidence and expertise. When answering questions related to your experience, begin your response with phrases such as "I know," "I've experienced," "In my work, I have," or "I've done." These sentence starters, and ones similar to them, will serve you well, reflect your experience, and continue to help build that relationship with the hiring manager and generate interest in who you are and what you do.

Be a diagnostic listener and listen for what they are looking for in a candidate and what they need. Be interested in what the interviewer has to say, rather than worrying about how interesting you are.

Always be mindful about how much you are speaking during an interview. Remember that a good interview is a robust dialogue between you and the hiring manager. If you believe you are talking too much, then you are. In general,

I coach my clients on keeping their answers to no longer than two minutes. Once you start speaking longer than that, you run the risk of losing the hiring manager's attention. If you find yourself talking too much, it's okay to pause and say something like, "I realize I said a lot there. Let me pause and check in with you to see if you have any follow-up questions." It can be easy to lose track of time when you are focused on sharing all of your experiences, background, and expertise to make sure the hiring manager knows you are a qualified candidate. While that's understandable, find a way to say all of that in a little less time and drive your point home.

8. **Ask thoughtful questions.**
Usually, at the end of the interview, you will get a chance to ask the hiring manager or panel questions. Know that the interviewer is taking note of the kinds of questions you ask. Avoid asking questions such as, "What's a typical day like?" or "What are the benefits?". Those are questions for another time. Ask questions you want to know about the company and

the position. This also may be an opportunity to ask a follow-up question based on something the interviewer asked you. Rely on your solid research to help create some great thought-provoking questions that reflect your interest in the position and organization. Your questions say a lot about you. This is another opportunity to build a memorable relationship with the hiring manager and interviewers.

9. **Answer the salary question decisively.**

If a company is seriously interested in hiring you, they may wonder if they can afford you. Just like answering the "Tell me about yourself" question, hiring managers and interviewers are specifically looking to see how you answer this question too. Let's acknowledge that this question causes practically everyone some amount of stress. Compensation is important. You never want to share a number that will feel like you are getting paid less than you are worth. Your experience and educational background are worth something. Make sure to do your research to determine what people in similar positions and industries are being paid.

Some common pitfalls to avoid when answering this question are asking another question such as "What's your budget?". You've deflected the question, and honestly, it doesn't make you look good. Additionally, be careful about giving a broad salary range. For example, if you gave a salary range between $90,000 and $100,000, wouldn't it make sense for the company to bring you in toward the lower end of that range? After all, they are a business. If they can get you toward the lower end of your range, on some level, it makes them look good. With that same example, if you are seeking $95,000, then say that. Be decisive in how you answer this question! This is your opportunity to be confident and give them a number. Let them counter. Now you can have a discussion. You will gauge whether or not your salary is more than what they were anticipating or in line. If you have done your work and built a memorable relationship with the hiring manager, this conversation will flow more easily. If you are asked what you are looking for regarding compensation, know your worth and value and decide if you are ready to share it with your potential employer.

Please note that in many states, it is illegal to request a candidate's current salary. According to a recent article by HRDive, "State and local governments are increasingly adopting laws and regulations that prohibit employers from requesting salary history information from job applicants. The laws are aimed at ending the cycle of pay discrimination and some go further than merely banning pay history questions. A few also prohibit an employer from relying on an applicant's pay history to set compensation if discovered or volunteered; others prohibit an employer from taking disciplinary action against employees who discuss pay with coworkers." I strongly encourage you to review your state and local laws regarding requesting salary history.

10. Make an agreement on the next steps.

This may be the most important thing you do during your interview. Making an agreement or setting ground rules about the next steps is vital to determining where you are in the process. It will also save you a lot of mind drama after you leave the interview. As the interview is wrapping up, the hiring manager or interviewer should give you some idea about their timeframe for selecting a candidate. They may say something like, "We expect to decide by a week from this Friday." You hear that and know what their expectations are for reaching a decision. You leave the interview, anxiously waiting for a week from Friday, only to hear nothing. You then spend the weekend wondering whether or not you got the job.

Hiring managers and recruiters are extremely busy. While it is always understood that they have the best intentions to meet the timeline they communicated, they may not. To save yourself from a lot of mind drama and wasting a lot of needless energy, it is appropriate for you to create an agreement about the next steps. I coach my clients on this every time they go for an interview. All of them come back and say that this strategy truly helped them SHOW

UP more energetically and build a better relationship with the hiring manager.

Here's how it works. The hiring manager says to you, "We expect to decide by a week from this Friday." You would say something like this, "That sounds great. I understand that things can get pretty busy, and there could be a possibility you may not decide by a week from this Friday. If I don't hear from you or someone on your team about a decision on my candidacy, may I contact you on the following Monday to inquire about my status?"

How the hiring manager answers your question will tell you everything. They will say that is fine, or they will say, "We will contact you." If they are not receptive to you following up if they miss their anticipated deadline, there is a strong likelihood that you are not the primary candidate considered for the position.

Given your career transition, you may be interviewing for multiple positions and may be juggling multiple offers. You ask this question and make agreements about the next steps solely so you and the hiring manager can establish definitive timelines.

BONUS TIP – Clients always ask me whether they should send a thank-you note after the interview. I firmly believe that sending a thank-you note is a great move. It is professional and it expresses your appreciation for everyone's time. However, with so many people working remotely, sending a handwritten thank-you note isn't logical because you don't have their home address and are uncertain when they are back in the office. It is appropriate and professional to send a thank-you email to everyone who interviewed you that day. If you don't have everyone's email address, email the hiring manager and let them know how much you appreciated everyone's time and highlight a particular point or takeaway from the interview. This is a great way to SHOW UP energetically, and whether or not you get the position, you showcase your best self in this process.

My 10 Interview Pet Peeves

1. **Lack of preparation.**
   It's a bad sign when a candidate comes into the interview and doesn't have a clear grasp of the position they are interviewing

for or knows what the company does. Time is precious. If the company has invested its time and energy to meet you, do your part and research the company and the position. You have spent a lot of time and energy to get the interview. Now, it's your time to SHOW UP energetically and professionally to do your best. Preparation is key.

2. **Answering questions too quickly or anticipating the question.**

   Interviews are a give-and-take. You get asked a question, and you respond. Be careful not to answer questions too quickly and make it sound like you have rehearsed every possible answer. Also, never interrupt the interviewer. Let them finish asking the question, and never anticipate or fill in their question for them. It makes it seem as if you are not listening to them and only focused on giving your answer. This can be a massive turnoff for many recruiters and hiring managers.

3. **Being vague or uncertain when it comes to why you want the position.**

   This is not the time to be coy when responding to why you are looking for a new position. There are ways to answer this question that makes you and everyone you work with and where you work look great. There is nothing to be ashamed about in improving yourself and advancing when those opportunities are not currently present in your organization. Everyone has had to work with the boss from hell. You don't want to say that during an interview. Never throw your boss, colleagues, or organization under the proverbial bus when you were interviewing because you are bitter or angry about your present situation. It is all about how you say it, and if you have had a problematic employment situation, coaching can certainly help.

   Additionally, many people lost their jobs due to the pandemic in 2020. Own that. If you were unfortunately laid off or furloughed because of the pandemic, good hiring managers and recruiters will understand what happened. They will be empathetic and understanding of where you are at in your career transition process.

4. **No personality or lack of personality.**
   It is perfectly natural to be nervous or on edge because this is an important interview for you. But you must show the interviewer you have a pulse! Let your verbal and nonverbal communication show you are interested. Be engaged in the conversation. Smile. Make good eye contact. If interviewing in person, give an appropriately firm handshake. Be engaged.

   Remember, aside from your technical expertise, the interviewer is trying to determine how well you will fit in with their team. If he/she can't get a good feeling about that, you failed at building the relationship.

   While it can be particularly challenging to show off your personality during a virtual interview, you still need to find a way to do that. A virtual interview doesn't give you an excuse to shut down or clam up when delivering your answers. Imagine as if that interviewer was sitting next to you. Envision yourself having a cup of coffee with them and having a great conversation. As I mentioned before, it is okay to be nervous, and a good hiring manager or interviewer will expect that at the start. But you need to get past it and focus on building that relationship and making a memorable impression.

5. **Not dressing appropriately.**

   I firmly believe it is better to be overdressed for the interview than underdressed. This is especially true in a virtual interview. Being appropriately dressed for an interview, and I mean the entire suit or outfit down to the shoes, will shift your energy and put you into the appropriate mindset and demonstrate your respect and importance for this interview. Make sure your suit/attire is neatly pressed and professional. No wrinkles or stains!

   We have all seen the viral videos of people having a Zoom fail where they weren't fully dressed for a meeting, exposing their shorts rather than their suit pants.

Interviews are not a time for you to be lazy. Be fully dressed. You'll be glad you did.

6. **Not being able to tell a clear story.**
   When answering interview questions that require you to tell a story, it's incredibly frustrating when a candidate cannot put clear thoughts together. Stories have a beginning, middle, and end. I have referenced using DDI's STAR method when responding to behavioral interview questions. A good hiring manager will be looking for your STAR components to your story. Make sure you communicate them.

7. **Using too many buzzwords or filler words.**
   Sometimes people think they need to drop the latest jargon or catchphrase in an interview. Be careful of that. For example, when people said I should hire them because they are a great team player, I always asked them to explain what they meant. The candidate assumes we have the same definition, but I don't know until I ask them for clarification. Be careful with your language. If you use a particular "buzzword," define it so everyone knows what you mean. Use filler words such as

"um," "like," "you know," and "so," judiciously and sporadically. Filler words can make it difficult to hear your message and make you sound like you don't have all of your thoughts together. Slow down. Think about what you are going to say. And say it clearly.

8. **Being lackluster at the virtual interview.** Because of the pandemic, practically every interview went virtual. And while people have experienced "Zoom Fatigue," you still need to SHOW UP and be great at the virtual interview. Not knowing how to work the technology ahead of time, being late for the interview, or having a poor camera or microphone makes you look bad. In 2021 and beyond, everyone has stepped up their game and created a great presence virtually. You need to do the same.

Additionally, 2020 saw an increase in companies using an interview platform where potential candidates recorded their answers and submitted them for review. This meant that candidates were answering questions without anyone on the other side of the screen. It was as if they were talking to no one. Yes, this is stressful, and if you are a perfectionist by nature, this kind of interview will probably drive you nuts. However, you need to be good at it. I have coached my clients on preparing for these types of interviews by setting up their phone or video camera and answering practice interview questions with no one on the other side. This helps them focus on their message, tell their story, communicate their unique professional value, and SHOW UP well on camera.

9. **Having no sense of humor.**
    Find some way to interject your sense of humor during the interview. Having a good laugh at something that happens or telling a funny story lets the interviewer know you are human and personable. If the interviewer makes a joke and you think it is funny, laugh. Remember that the interview is a dialogue between the both of you. Be personable. It's okay.

10. Not following up.

After the interview is over, make sure to send a "thank-you" message. Acknowledge and thank those you met and share something about what you learned or were impressed by during your interview. This also is an opportunity to share something you may have missed during the interview. Not following up is missing a chance to let them know how much you appreciated their time and the opportunity to interview for the position. Remember, interviewing is about building a relationship and getting them *interested* in who you are and what you do. Whether you are selected for the position or not, don't miss this important step. After all, if you want the job, wouldn't you want to make a good impression?

How Do You Prepare for an Interview?

There is no way to prepare for every interview question. To try only results in creating an impossible level of stress over figuring out what questions they will ask and how you should respond. You may care so much about doing well that you think this is the best way to prepare. In reality, it only causes you to worry and waste a lot of energy. That's why I coach my clients on having five powerful stories they can access to answer any interview question.

There is no way to prepare for every interview question. To try only results in creating an impossible level of stress over figuring out what questions they will ask and how you should respond.

According to Drexel University's LeBow College of Business, there are various types of interviews. The first is the traditional interview. Think of this as you meeting with one person and answering a series of questions related to the job. Usually, another interview is scheduled when you move to the next round. The interview can cover various technical and behavioral questions. Also, panel interviews may fall under this traditional style of interview, during which you are asked questions from a team of two or more interviewers.

A behavioral interview is when you are asked questions directly related to your experience. Questions such as "Tell me about a time when" or

"Given your experience" are common. With these types of questions, you will want to use DDI's STAR method to frame your response.

A technical interview will focus more on your educational background and relevant experience regarding specific skills needed to perform the job successfully. Here, you may be asked about particular software or programs you are proficient in using or particular skills you use in your work.

How Have Interviews Changed Because of the Pandemic?

Virtual interviews are never going away. From the company's standpoint, this saves them a lot of money because they no longer have to fly candidates in for a full-day interview unless they are sure they would be an excellent fit for such a position. We've talked about having a good camera and microphone, as well as testing the technology before your interview. More importantly, I believe everyone should be prepared to answer specific questions about the pandemic and how you used your time during the quarantine. Be ready to answer questions related to what you learned during the pandemic. 2020 saw an uptick in online learning through LinkedIn

Learning, Udemy, or Coursera with people looking to enhance their professional development. How did you take advantage of these opportunities?

You also should be prepared to address how you work virtually. How did you manage your time not being in the office? What things have worked well for you in a virtual environment, and where did you have to adapt? What programs or platforms did you get to use, such as Zoom, Microsoft Teams, Slack, Skype, Dropbox, Google Docs, Google Slides, and Google Forms? People will be curious to know how you adapted your work-life balance and found ways to be more productive given how difficult working remotely can be without the nuances of being at the worksite.

Not everyone is well versed in working remotely. For many people in 2020 who envisioned or thought about being a remote worker, this was "fun" for a few weeks. As weeks turned into months and dining room tables became makeshift home offices, the fun wore off pretty quickly. These are the experiences you will need to draw upon in sharing what it's been like for you to work remotely. Perhaps you are fortunate enough to have a dedicated home office, and thus, the shift to working remotely wasn't as tricky from a technical standpoint. Still, you missed the camaraderie and collegiality of seeing your team members and colleagues every day. There is no question that 2020 changed the way we worked. Think about how its impact affected you and has helped you change direction on Your Mid-Career GPS.

Some Final Thoughts on Promoting Who You Are and What You Do

Your Mid-Career GPS has taken you on some exciting roads and maybe a few detours along the way. Where you are right now, as you read this book, is because of the totality of your experiences. Those experiences shape who you are and what you do.

Talking about yourself is never easy for heart-centered leaders and professionals, but building relationships are. For you, coming from a place of value and service is vital to building such connections. You have something that can help a new company or organization. You bring a collection of desperately needed skills, but you must find a way to tell your story and share what you can do with the world. Let's use the following questions to help you sum up what we've covered in this chapter.

What are five stories that best describe your value and accomplishments in your work/career?
1.
2.
3.
4.
5.

Write your response to how you would answer the "Tell me about yourself" question. Use your UPVS as part of your response.

What is one thing you know you can do confidently in an interview?

What is one thing you need to work on so you can do it confidently in an interview?

Chapter 4

SHOW UP –
Let's Put This to Work
#SHOWUP6Strategies

As your trip through this book begins to wind down, it's important to remember to stay hyper-focused. Keep your attention on your destination as you hold onto all of the momentum you have generated in the first three parts to building Your Mid-Career GPS. This part is my favorite because it will unlock many answers and help you navigate the road ahead. We need to talk about what it means for you to SHOW UP.

When I wrote my first book, "SHOW UP – Six Strategies to Lead a More Energetic and Impactful Career," it was a personal account of a memorable life event that happened to me when I was 10 years old that set the stage for how I was expected to SHOW UP in my life. The book is part memoir and part tactical guide to help you navigate various aspects of your career. The book was published in April 2020 and received fantastic reviews about how it helped people think a little differently about their careers and their lives.

For me, how I SHOW UP in my life and career is not only important to me, but also, it's my mission. The six strategies I outlined in my book have been guiding principles to help me handle any personal or professional situation I face. Whenever I question what to do, I think about how I want to SHOW UP.

My #SHOWUP6Strategies are:
- Set ground rules.
- Have intentional conversations.
- Own where you are.
- Welcome new opportunities.
- Use your genius.
- Protect and promote your brand.

How we choose to SHOW UP has been a consistent theme in my coaching relationships. My coaching clients are very familiar with my #SHOWUP6Strategies. I use that hashtag whenever I post on social media so people can see how adaptive and multifaceted these strategies are. My #SHOWUP6Strategies serve as a conversation starter across the organizational chart.

One of my coaching clients, Jennifer Miller, who works for a Fortune 50 company as an outstanding project manager and leader, recently shared these thoughts after completing my #SHOWUPChallenge.

Jennifer wrote, "Learning how to 'SHOW UP' with intention is the most powerful tool I've ever learned, and I use it in all aspects of my life. It makes me a stronger employee, leader, peer, wife, daughter, sister, friend, etc. It is an empowerment that I never knew I was missing and has provided me with a confidence that I have difficulty describing. However, even my husband has commented on the benefits he sees my coaching sessions have provided, and there is zero question whether or not the financial investment is worth it. I dare say that this investment has brought me more benefit than any cost I've spent on a formal education such as my MBA."

I am humbled and grateful for the glowing reviews this book and my coaching programs have received. As you are building Your Mid-Career GPS, you must remember that your journey is personal. While this book has provided you with various strategic and tactical guidance to help you prepare, position, and promote who you are and what you do, neglecting to have a conversation about what it means for you to SHOW UP would be a huge mistake on my part.

My first podcast, #SHOWUP2020, highlighted everyday people doing extraordinary things because of how they choose to SHOW UP. I welcomed healthcare professionals, public servants, people who found jobs during the pandemic, teachers and educational leaders, entrepreneurs, and mid-career professionals much like yourself who came on air to share their stories and lessons learned that 2020 showed them how they responded to it. I am beyond grateful to all my guests who took the time to share their stories on my podcast. But one of the things that came out of those conversations was how all of them had a personal career GPS in some shape or form. Whether they realized it or not, they navigated, pivoted, and maneuvered various situations to move their career forward, demonstrate leadership, and SHOW UP as their authentic selves to get the work done. They are amazing people with tremendous stories. I hope you will take the time to listen to them.

In this chapter, you will:
- Learn what each of my #SHOWUP6Strategies means to you and how you are applying them to your professional life.
- Determine which strategy, or strategies, deserve your greatest attention to help you navigate your career transition.
- Focus on using these #SHOWUP6Strategies to help you find the job you love or love the job you have.

As your read this section, please note I listed these strategies in order of relevance and importance to building Your Mid-Career GPS and not in order of the acronym. I did this to help you take a more strategic look at how these strategies can help you as you figure out whatever is next for your career. Remember – how you SHOW UP matters. Let's get started.

Own Where You Are –
How the Pandemic Held a Mirror Up to Our Faces
and Forced Us to Look into It.

Looking in the mirror and being brutally honest with yourself without being judgmental is one of the hardest things you will ever do. Taking an assessment of what's working and what's not in your career is one of the best ways to accept where you are, give yourself some grace, and plan some action about what you want to do. Your career consists of many chapters as you learn to tell and develop your stories. That's why Owning Where You Are is one of the most pivotal parts of creating Your Mid-Career GPS. Once you honestly and authentically look at yourself in the mirror, extraordinary things begin to happen.

Earlier in the book, I mentioned that we all have that "mid-career moment." Those moments help you identify where you are professionally and decide what actions you want to take. It can be challenging to look in the mirror without judgment and assess what's working well and what isn't. As I shared in the Prepare section, your inner critic may be speaking to you pretty loudly. How you address your inner critic and process what it is saying reflects your life and career ownership.

Ownership is about taking inventory. Sometimes you enlist the help of trusted colleagues and critical friends to create a more accurate picture of yourself as you build Your Mid-Career GPS. One of my favorite books is "With Winning in Mind" by Lanny Bassham. Lanny is a two-time Olympic medalist and the creator and owner of Mental Management Systems. As Lanny trained for Olympic competitions, he asked himself three pivotal questions to assess the quality of his training sessions to focus on what he learned. Those three questions are:

- What did I do well?
- What did I learn?
- What do I need to work on?

Being coached by Lanny's daughter, Heather Sumlin, who helped me tremendously with my mental game for bowling out on the PBA tour, I quickly learned these questions were phenomenal questions that can be used outside of competition. When I started asking my clients these questions, it helped them assess where they were in their careers and opened their minds to look at their experiences more from data points than critical lenses.

You need opportunities like that. To truly take ownership of where you are in your career, you need to stop lying to yourself. If you are disappointed you didn't get the promotion, I encourage you to get the necessary feedback you need to learn from that. If you didn't get the raise you wanted, I invite you to examine your worth and value in the marketplace and determine what is holding you back from asking for precisely what it is you want. If you are dealing with a difficult team member or boss, this is an excellent opportunity for you to look at the situation in terms of what you have direct control over and what you don't. Look at that relationship and own what parts of it you are directly responsible for.

Because of the pandemic, I often say that we were given a chance to get off the hamster wheel and evaluate where we were with our careers and lives. While this is more of a career and leadership coaching book than it is about life coaching, I'd be remiss to say that there are times when these coaching niches overlap. How did the pandemic help you reevaluate where your career was headed? How did COVID-19 directly affect you? Did you lose a family member, close friend, or loved one to this deadly disease? If you did, I'm genuinely sorry for your loss. My family of choice lost someone to COVID-19 early during the pandemic. It certainly made us reevaluate things.

Because of the pandemic,
I often say that we were given a chance
to get off the hamster wheel and evaluate
where we were with our careers and lives.

One of the most potent phrases coming out of the pandemic has been "Build Back Better." According to Wikipedia, the origination for "Build Back Better" was first described in the United Nations Framework for Disaster Risk Reduction. "Building Back Better (BBB) is a strategy aimed at reducing the risk to the people of nations and communities in the wake of future disasters and shocks."

From my purview, you can't begin to "Build Back Better" unless you Own Where You Are. When building Your Mid-Career GPS, everything you do originates from this point. This is where your journey begins as you navigate toward whatever is next. Ownership is key. Take the time to look into the proverbial or actual mirror and take stock of where you are. Ask yourself what is working, what isn't working, what you have learned, and how you will take all that information and put it into Your Mid-Career GPS so you can find a job you love or love the job you have.

What's working well for you professionally?

What's not working well for you professionally?

What do you want to learn to help better your position in the marketplace?

Welcome New Opportunities and What We've Learned from the Pandemic.

You will seek new opportunities throughout your career because you want to "move up the ladder" or "get ahead" to get the promotion, earn more money, and have more responsibilities. Yet, you can welcome many more opportunities, ranging from learning a new facet of your job to developing new skills. Being open to such opportunities comes from your mindset. Welcoming new opportunities is your gateway to continued growth, mobility, and career success and must be an integral strategy in building Your Mid-Career GPS.

Given the severity of the pandemic and its impact on small businesses and specific industries such as transportation, hospitality, food service, and retail, it would be understandable and necessary to spend some time and grieve for what used to be and be disappointed with our current reality. I had three guests on my podcast, #SHOWUP2020, who found new jobs during the pandemic. They were able to do that because they created a mindset focused on their value, identified where they were needed and how they were going to serve, and remained resilient throughout their entire career transition process. Was it challenging to find a new job in 2020? Absolutely! Nevertheless, some people did and were able to find their dream jobs and create wonderful new opportunities because they were not willing to settle for anything less.

In her book, "Mindset: The New Psychology of Success," Carol Dweck writes, "The passion for stretching yourself and sticking to it, even (or especially) when it's not going well, is the hallmark of the growth mindset. This is the mindset that allows people to thrive during some of the most challenging times in their lives."

It is without question that many career professionals, as well as business owners, found themselves at a critical juncture because of the pandemic. As a former educator, the thought of teaching remotely was immediately dismissed as something that wouldn't work years ago. As I have followed the news and spoken with dozens of educators and educational leaders across the country, it is in my opinion that remote learning, while able to work in some districts, isn't an ideal or universal solution, and we have the evidence to prove that. However, districts moved to remote or hybrid learning out of an abundance of caution, not just for students, teachers, and staff, but also for their communities. I do not know of one teacher who prefers remote learning over in-person instruction. Given the pandemic, the opportunity presented to many educators, students, and families was to find ways to balance learning remotely amid the pressures of remote work to ensure that kids learned and adults could get their work completed.

Companies and their executives who were reluctant or hesitant to allow a large portion of their workforce to be remote were faced with an opportunity in 2020 they could not avoid. Many companies moved to work remotely despite their wishes or interests to ensure safety and maintain social distancing.

In an article for Fast Company, Greg Caplan, the CEO of Remote Year, stated, "Coronavirus is going to expose more people to working remotely than ever... most people will say that it is possible and start to grow accustomed to the benefits of [remote work], including autonomy, no commute, and fewer distractions than open offices. Companies that don't allow remote work already are going to have to continue supporting it going forward, now that they have proven to themselves that it works."

I never worked remotely until the last 10 years, and the majority of that was a sporadic day here or there when I had a doctor's appointment or a repair going on at the house, and it was just easier for me to be home and flextime to get my work done. When I decided to launch my coaching practice full time, I wondered what working from home full time would be like. As someone who thrives being around people and enjoys the noise and energy of either being in a school or working in an office, I had my concerns or reservations about how well I would thrive in this new environment. What I learned by welcoming this new opportunity is that I love it!

As you build Your Mid-Career GPS, there is tremendous value in listening, leaning in, and stepping toward the opportunities you want to welcome. Depending on where you are in your career, you may be asking yourself, when is enough really enough? You may have had that moment or are waiting to have that moment when you realize where you are no longer serves you or is in your best interest. As I was preparing to leave my last position, a dear colleague and friend told me that changing jobs or careers was like looking for a bigger pair of jeans. While I had done excellent work, my jeans were just getting a little too tight, and I was ready to level up to a bigger size. Honestly, I think that's the only time I have ever enjoyed fitting into a bigger pair of jeans.

As you build Your Mid-Career GPS, there is
tremendous value in listening,
leaning in, and stepping toward the
opportunities you want to welcome.

While it is one thing to accept the status quo, when you are ready to welcome a new opportunity, recognize that it is time for a change. You are prepared to acknowledge that there are bigger opportunities out there for you, and now, as you build Your Mid-Career GPS, it is time to go after them.

Identifying these opportunities typically happens toward the end of the preparing stage and the beginning of the positioning stages in building Your Mid-Career GPS. Once you are clear about how you want to level up or make a horizontal move to either get out of a current situation or get your foot in the door at another organization, you will welcome these opportunities. Creating a greater awareness around these opportunities is just one of the many ways you will SHOW UP in your career. Acknowledge your thoughts. They are the key to helping you welcome any new opportunity.

What opportunities are in front of you that you want to welcome and go after to help you figure out whatever is next for you and your career?

Why Setting Ground Rules is One of the Best Things You Will Ever Do in Your Career (or Life).

I have said this for years - when you set ground rules, you know how to play, and when you know how to play, there is never any doubt on how to navigate a situation. Heart-centered leaders sometimes have difficulty setting ground rules or norms. They are often too concerned or hyper-focused on ensuring everyone is happy. Doing this holds them back from SHOWing UP as the leaders they are called to be. That's why setting ground rules is essential for building highly effective and productive teams who are on board with sharing the organization's or company's vision. Ground rules help us create greater unity, continuity, and community at work and on our teams.

While ground rules can help build teams, let's focus on how ground rules can help you SHOW UP professionally in your career. During your preparation stage, you gained clarity about your attitudes and strengths and began to consider your value for whatever is next for your career. Previously, I shared a job search strategy that may be helpful to reduce some overwhelm and stress. You may set a ground rule reflecting your commitment to that job search process. For example, you may say, "Mondays and Wednesdays are my days to look for new positions. Tuesdays and Thursdays are my days to apply for those positions."

You may set a ground rule for how you communicate your UVPS when networking or interviewing. That ground rule may be, "I will energetically share my value at this networking event with 10 people. I will not question my value and I will share it from a place where I can help someone. I am committed to my GPS."

Other examples of ground rules include:
- "I always produce quality work."
- "I keep a growth mindset."
- "I am always working to improve my skills."
- "I will apply for five jobs in the next two weeks."
- "I will focus on listening to my team members rather than immediately interjecting a solution."

Setting ground rules help you set intentions for what you want to do and who you want to be. One of the most significant ways to improve your professional trajectory and build meaningful components to Your Mid-Career GPS is to work on your thoughts. According to Brooke Castillo from The Life Coach School, our thoughts create feelings, which create actions, which ultimately produce results. So it makes sense that your ground rules help shape your mindset for how you want to SHOW UP.

Setting ground rules help you set intentions for what you want to do and who you want to be.

As you increase your awareness about your thoughts and use them to set ground rules, you can adopt a mindset that helps you stretch and evolve into the professional you want to be. Once again, citing Carol Dweck from her book, "Mindset: The New Psychology of Success," she states, "Mindset change is not about picking up a few pointers here and there. It's about seeing things in a new way. When people...change to a growth mindset, they change from a judge-and-be-judged framework to a learn-and-help-learn framework. Their commitment is to growth, and growth takes plenty of time, effort, and mutual support."

While mindset work is essential to setting ground rules, holding yourself accountable to honoring them may be different. Having an accountability partner may be a great addition to helping you SHOW UP in various situations and processing what you have learned. In an article for Inc.com in June 2020, titled, "Three Tried and True Ways to Hold Yourself Accountable," Jon Levy recommends finding someone you trust who you can be accountable to. This will help build momentum and keep you focused on whatever goals, or ground rules, you have set for yourself. Levy also recommends finding ways to increase accountability when you are at your strongest or have significant momentum. He refers to this as the Ulysses Pact. Levy writes, "As important as it is to set goals, it is essential for us to be accountable for those goals. The fact is that none of us are as productive as we want to be." This is where enlisting the help of an accountability partner can be a great asset to your career growth.

Lastly, there is one memory from 2020 I must call out because, for me, it's an important example of how we SHOW UP by setting ground rules. During the 2020 Vice-Presidential Debate, Senator Kamala Harris repeatedly told Vice-President Mike

Pence, "I'm speaking." For me, this was a perfect example of setting a ground rule and honoring it.

During the first presidential debate, both candidates repeatedly interrupted and talked over each other. Going into the only Vice Presidential Debate, there was an expectation that both candidates would be more respectful of the debate rules and participate in a more structured debate. Early in the debate, when Senator Harris was speaking, Vice President Pence interjected. She looked at him and calmly and confidently said, "I'm speaking." Though she repeated it several times, to me, it was apparent this was a ground rule she established for herself in SHOWing UP for this debate. I'm willing to bet she had accountability partners help her with this. After all, imagine being able to report back that you honored your ground rule and did so in the way you intended.

A CNBC article by Courtney Connley cites that "In the recent survey of 1,100 U.S. working adults over the age of 18, Catalyst, a nonprofit that works to accelerate women into leadership, found that 45% of women business leaders say it's difficult for women to speak up in virtual meetings and one in five women say they've felt ignored or overlooked by colleagues during video calls."

We create ground rules because they help us SHOW UP in energetically and powerfully confident ways to honor our intentions. You get to set whatever ground rules you want for your career and your professional development. Know that as you create Your Mid-Career GPS, ground rules will play an integral part in helping you prepare, position, and promote who you are and what you do so you can find a job you love or love the job you have.

You get to set whatever ground rules
you want for your career
and your professional development.

What is one ground rule you will set that you believe will help you in your career?

Why do you believe the ground rule you mentioned above will help you?

The Power of Having Intentional Conversations.

It's understandable why people shy away from certain types of conversations. They may be afraid of rejection, being told "no," not getting a raise or promotion, or getting exactly what they ask for. Conflict doesn't have to be complicated and filled with a lot of drama. Our brains love to take us places where we envision various scenarios that can sometimes create a lot of undue stress. There is an art to having an intentional conversation, and the sole purpose is to move that relationship forward.

I want you to imagine two chairs, sitting side by side. Imagine sitting in one of those chairs and inviting someone to sit in the chair next to you. This could be your boss, supervisor, direct report, a trusted colleague, a coworker with whom you had a disagreement, a dear friend, or a loved one. You invite them to take a seat. As you're sitting next to them, you begin to share your well-rehearsed and practiced introduction to this conversation. You may be feeling a little nervous or uneasy about what you have to talk about, but you know it's imperative to have this conversation. As you begin talking, imagine how you are feeling. Think about the physical, as well as the emotional, response you are having in this conversation. As you watch this person's reaction, note how they are processing the information you share with them. Are they happy? Are they disappointed or angry? How will you react to their emotions? How will you keep the dialogue moving? How does the conversation end? Have you created the next steps for a follow-up conversation or not? After the conversation is over, how do you feel? Do you feel as if you could vomit, or do you have this huge sense of relief after having the conversation and knowing it is finished?

Remember, the goal for any intentional conversation is to move that relationship forward. This means, by the time that conversation is finished, you and that other person have grown because of what you shared.

Remember, the goal for any intentional conversation is to move that relationship forward.

Intentional conversations are not always easy, nor are they always intended to have the outcome you desire. Intentional conversations are not designed to make you feel better. Once you have identified who you need to talk to, and have planned what you want to say, set a goal for what you hope the outcome will be.

In my first book, I shared an intentional conversation I had with my vice president shortly before leaving that job to open my coaching practice full time. Talking about your career path isn't always easy. After surviving two re-organizations, I landed in what I'd like to describe as a less than optimal place but was exceptionally grateful I still had a job. Being very clear about my coaching ambitions and what I wanted to do within the organization, I had an intentional conversation with my vice president to clarify where my standing was within the company and to help me make some informed decisions about my next step. Getting confirmation that I was right and doing good work was wonderful, but learning that my coaching ambitions within the company wouldn't be met or there was little path for me moving upward was not easy to hear. But I got the information I needed. When you have an intentional conversation and get enough information to help you move forward, that is a success.

Leaving a company to advance your career or accept a better offer that aligns with Your Mid-Career GPS is never easy when you work with great people and enjoy what you get to do every day. As Shari Harley states in her book, "How to Say Anything to Anyone," "You are 100% responsible for your career." I love this line from her book. It has been a constant reminder that I am the only one responsible for the decisions I make in my career, and I got this.

Everyone can benefit from learning to be a better communicator. Part of my expertise has always been having difficult conversations when needed. It doesn't mean that I enjoy them or have always been good at delivering them. Giving and receiving feedback is an art. Shari Harley emphasizes that feedback should be provided for two reasons: "Maintaining behavior or shifting behavior."

Another fantastic component from Sheri Harley's book is her "Eight Steps to Say Anything to Anyone in Two Minutes or Fewer." Her feedback protocol includes: "Introduce the conversation, empathize, describe the observed behavior, share the impact or result, have some dialogue, make a suggestion or request, build agreement on next steps, and say thank you."

I read her entire book on a cross-country flight several years ago. To date, it is still one of the best business leadership books I have ever read. Giving feedback is certainly one component or aspect of having intentional conversations.

You may consider networking or interviewing as having intentional conversations. How is your relationship better because of that conversation with someone at a networking event or during an interview? How is that person better by meeting you and vice versa? Never underestimate the impact you can have on someone, whether it be for a few minutes or years working alongside them.

Who is one person you'd like to have an intentional conversation with about your career and your career path?

Why is that person the right person to have an intentional conversation with right now?

What do you hope to learn or gain from that conversation?

Why Now is the Perfect Time to Use Your Genius

All of us are given individual gifts, but we are called to use our genius to serve others. Throughout our careers, there are times when our passion or love for what we do wanes. Maybe right now you are feeling stuck or unhappy in your career. The key to shifting those feelings is to find a job where you can leverage your talents and expertise. When you can do this, you see where you "fit."

We've discussed "fit" in a previous section and how it's essential to developing Your Mid-Career GPS. When you think about your genius, I want you to connect that to your UPVS, but take it one step further. Think about your value statement and recognize that while many people can do what you do, only you can bring that certain "something" to the position. Your genius is what sets you apart from everyone else.

When you think about your genius,
I want you to connect that to your UPVS,
but take it one step further.

This became very clear to me when I was a middle school mathematics teacher. I worked in a fantastic school district alongside some amazingly talented mathematics teachers. I learned from them and was motivated by them. And while there were things that I brought into my instruction, based on my experience and genius, I knew hundreds of people actively applied for teaching positions every year. I know any one of those people could've stepped in and did a good job or maybe even a better job teaching my students than I did. I needed to realize that when I use my genius, I can do my job in my unique way based on the value I bring to that position.

When I work with my coaching clients, we identify their genius in conjunction with their UPVS. I ask them who loses out when you don't use your genius. This is one of those coaching questions that makes them stop and think. They have to reflect on how extraordinary they are. They have to recall their relationships, work, and why what they bring to that position makes them stand out above everyone else. I have had clients get incredibly creative when describing their UPVS and have shared them at networking events and interviews. They have reported back how memorable those moments are and how, just by sharing their genius in that way, it shifted the dynamic during those conversations for the better.

Your genius is your gift. When you hold back from sharing your genius, either within your organization or people on your team, you do not give them the whole experience of working with you and learning from you. Know that this works both ways. Once you have identified your genius, find opportunities where you can enhance or strengthen your genius. Referring back to the Gallup Clifton StrengthsFinder Assessment, it is in your best interest to continually develop your top five strengths to give you the greatest chance of career happiness, productivity, and "fit."

You can synonymously connect your genius with your unique professional value. Consider asking yourself, "How would you show up if you knew your value was non-negotiable?"

No one else has your genius. No one.

What is your genius?

(Think about your UPVS and expand on it. How does your value connect to your genius?)

Why Protecting and Promoting Your Brand is Vital to Creating Your Mid-Career GPS.

Brands are not reserved for large companies. You have a brand. When you think of yourself as a brand, your mindset shifts to greater awareness about what you are putting out into the world and what others say about you. Many people would prefer to focus on their reputation rather than their brand. While both are important, until you are clear about your brand, you cannot fully SHOW UP in ways that demonstrate your value and service. Your genius is one component to helping you identify why your brand is valuable.

Kimberly Schneiderman, in her article for Randstad titled, "5 Tips to Boost Your Personal and Professional Brand," states, "Your brand is what makes you unique—it's what makes you, you. It's an authentic representation of who you are as a person and as a professional. It's tied to your identity and encompasses the emotional connection you have with your career path. The better able you are to create a personal and professional brand, the more likely you are to achieve success along the way."

In building Your Mid-Career GPS, you have spent this entire book collectively examining what your brand is. It is the perfect strategy to close this section. As Jeff Bezos, Founder of Amazon, says, "Your brand is what people say about you when you're not in the room." If you are not aware of your brand, my advice is to ask trusted colleagues and close friends what they believe your brand is. Your brand should reflect your values, strengths, and attitudes, along with your skills, representing who you are and what you do. Your reputation is how well you deliver on your brand.

Recently, I had a conversation with a new connection from my local Chamber of Commerce. When she asked me what I do, I shared my UPVS and emphasized a few more points I believed would help our conversation. She nodded her head and told me that what I had just shared was directly in line with what she understands of me on LinkedIn. That was important because it confirmed that my brand messaging is consistent.

Think of promoting your brand as an opportunity to share or demonstrate your unique professional value. As I coach clients on preparing for a promotion, one of the biggest misconceptions some professionals believe is that time spent doing a particular job is grounds for earning a promotion. Nothing could be further from the truth.

Think of promoting your brand as an opportunity to share or demonstrate your unique professional value.

You are ready for a promotion when you have demonstrated the necessary skills, competencies, and abilities for the level you are trying to obtain. I coach my clients on creating a mindset and work ethic that reflects how they would SHOW UP if they were already in that role. For example, if you are trying to become a director in your company, what skills are needed at the director level? How can your work reflect director-quality results?

At some point in our mid-career journey, it seems as if we forget what it was like when we were fresh out of college. Back then, we were hungry to do excellent work and always wanted to put our best foot forward. Now, at mid-career, it's understandable we may become complacent doing the same job after so many years. Your brand is not something you turn off and on. Your brand is a reflection of who you are as a professional. We all want to be known for doing quality work. However, what we must remember, in the words of Maya Angelou, is, "People will forget what you said, people will forget what you did, but people will never forget how you made them feel."

Think not only about what you want to be known for but also for how you want to be remembered. The legacy you create is a direct reflection of your professional and personal brand.

There are times when you need to protect your brand. This is more about managing your reputation and having your finger on the pulse about what people say about you and the work you are doing. I invite you to solicit feedback from people other than your immediate supervisor. Find that trusted colleague or critical friend who you can ask specific, intentional questions about your brand and reputation. If there is an opportunity or need to do damage control, then do it. We are not perfect people. We are human, and we are flawed. Maybe you had a lousy client meeting, or you facilitated a presentation that went sideways. These things will happen. Learn from it and protect your brand.

If you are looking for some guidance, here are some branding questions to help you get the conversation started. Find a trusted colleague and record their answers.

How would you define my professional brand?

What are three things you recognize about my work?

What three values do you see me demonstrate every day?

What's one thing you believe I should improve upon to be a better leader, employee, or project manager?

If you were to tell someone about me, what would you say?

Final Thoughts About #SHOWUP6Strategies

My #SHOWUP6Strategies are a tactical and strategic guide to help you SHOW UP in your career. These strategies are applicable throughout your career and serve as a constant reminder to define how you choose to SHOW UP more clearly.

We see the words "show up" often in conversations, books, and social media. Part of my mission is to help normalize the conversation around what it means to SHOW UP, and let my books serve as guides to help professionals define what that means to them at any stage of their career.

These are not revolutionary or earth-shattering strategies. Throughout my career, these strategies, whether they have been obvious or not, have served me well in navigating through multiple organizations and several career advancements; building and repairing teams; delivering relevant, timely, and helpful feedback; and making my impact wherever I had an opportunity to work and serve.

Since my first book's release, I have used #SHOWUP6Strategies in over 500 posts. Yes, it is part of my brand. When you have done something that aligns with one of these strategies and are inclined to post on social media, I hope you tag #SHOWUP6Strategies. Tag me in those posts. Share with me and others what you have learned and what these strategies mean to you. I would not be where I am today if it weren't for these strategies aligned to my Mid-Career GPS. My Mid-Career GPS, like yours, is personal. Even my business has a GPS. I'm executing it sometimes flawlessly, and sometimes it's a little messy. And that's okay. I just know that without question, based on the ground rules I set for myself, I know how I want to SHOW UP and do that. I wish you the best in your endeavors as well.

Remember – how you SHOW UP matters.

Which SHOW UP strategy do you want to work on immediately?

How will working on that strategy help you in your career?

Remember – how you SHOW UP matters.

My Closing Letter to You

Dear Reader,

Now that you have finished my book, I want to leave you with a few closing thoughts. As you have worked through this book's information to build Your Mid-Career GPS, I hope you have greater clarity about who you are and what you do. Building your mid-career roadmap is not all about finding the perfect job. This book has been part of your journey to explore who you are at this stage in your career.

Now your résumé should be a direct reflection of your accomplishments and recognition of your career to date. Your LinkedIn accurately reflects the value you bring to anyone you connect with and where you work. Be known as someone who networks from a place of service. Value being a connector before asking for anything for yourself first. The next time you go to an interview, recognize that you have an incredible story to tell. Never shy away from communicating your experiences and talents and why someone needs them because you are the right person to help solve their problems as described in the job posting. You've taken time to explore your attitudes, strengths, and values. Always make sure they are reflected in what you write and how you talk about yourself.

As you build Your Mid-Career GPS, I hope you see the importance of what it means for you to SHOW UP. SHOWing UP is about the energy you bring to situations. It is how you connect, lead, and make the impact you want, no matter who you are talking to or where you work. How you SHOW UP evolves just as much as how you build your skills and talents. As you move toward the later stages of your career, I hope you will take all of the lessons you've learned throughout your career and from this book to help shape whatever is next for you.

Your Mid-Career GPS is guiding you on this journey. It's flexible. Sometimes detours happen that you didn't expect, but they are there for a reason. Enjoy the ride because it's an amazing experience. As you look back at all you did, what you are doing, and what you will do, I wish you nothing but the utmost happiness, joy, and satisfaction. You have affected and will continue to affect a lot of people along the way. It is your gift to the world.

Remember - how you SHOW UP matters.

With love,
John

Acknowledgments

When I decided to write another book shortly after the release of "SHOW UP – Six Strategies to Lead a More Energetic and Impactful Career," I honestly thought I was crazy. But 2020 was a memorable year given the pandemic, racial injustice, record unemployment, food insecurities, and a heightened desire to live the life you've always dreamed of. When you are called to do something, you listen, and you decide whether or not this is the right thing to do. I'm glad I answered that call.

For fear of missing anyone on this list after reviewing it multiple times, know that I appreciate your love, support, encouragement, and guidance to help make this book the best tactical guide to help people navigate their careers, whether in 2021 or down the road.

Richard – Without your love and support, none of this would be possible. Thank you for the many conversations we had over meals, in the car, at night, wherever, when I wouldn't stop talking about this book. As a loving husband and confidant, you have listened and guided me as the wonderful man you are. I'm blessed beyond words to have you by my side.

Mike – Going through coach training with you at iPEC (Institute for Professional Excellence in Coaching) was a blast, but our friendship is deeply appreciated. Thank you for introducing me to Andrea Seydel. You were correct – the energy was something else, and I'm grateful to have had the chance to meet her and work with her because you made that connection for us.

Andrea – You are a fantastic book coach who helped me create a process far different than my last book. You had all of the right questions to ask to help me get the words on these pages and share my message with the world. It's been a pleasure to partner with you and Live Life Happy Publishing.

To my Editorial Board – Alethea, Brian, Dean, D'Ivonne, Jennifer, and Jessi – I couldn't have asked for a better group to serve on this board. Your insight, feedback, and thoughts made revising this book more effortless, and I know, without question, that this version is far better than if I had done this on my own. All of you are amazingly talented and dedicated professionals, and I'm blessed to know each of you.

Natalie – I'm honored and grateful you took the time to write the foreword. Your friendship has been one of the greatest gifts at this stage in my life. Seeing your progress is an inspiration.

Rich – You are an outstanding editor, and I'm grateful for our friendship and collegiality. Your ability to see this editorial process through facilitating an extraordinary board meeting has tremendously helped make this book what it is. Thank you.

To Bruce D Schneider and the entire team at iPEC – I can't begin to thank you enough for sharing your knowledge, training, experiences, and insights to help me be the best coach I can be. I am beyond grateful for every one of you.

To my fellow coaches – We get to do the work we do because we profoundly believe in helping our clients lead better lives and careers. Thank you for the conversations that have helped me grow as a coach and better serve my clients.

To my clients – Having an opportunity to coach you has been one of my greatest joys in my career. I'm proud of you for the work you have done to get you where you are today. I appreciate your unapologetically fearless attitude to create the results you want as you continue to chart that path toward creating your personal and professional legacy. Your insight and dedication are inspirational.

About the Author

John Neral is an executive and career transition coach who helps mid-career professionals prepare, position, and promote who they are and what they do to SHOW UP and find a job they love or love the job they have. John is a celebrated and recognized speaker who delivers keynotes, workshops, seminars, and trainings to organizations, companies, and teams across the country on various leadership and career topics.

Listen to "The Mid-Career GPS Podcast" on your favorite listening platform or at https://johnneral.com. You are welcome to join John's private Facebook Group called "Your Mid-Career GPS" and join a like-minded group of professionals who are actively building their roadmaps to help them get to whatever is next for them professionally.

John is an avid game show enthusiast and professional bowler. Having visited five of the seven continents, he is always looking for his next great travel adventure. He is happily married, and he and his spouse are the proud parents of a rescue cat named Amy Farrah Meowler because of their love of "The Big Bang Theory."

Visit https://johnneral.com for more information, and the free resources for this book. You can email John at john@johnneral.com. Connect with John on LinkedIn or Facebook and Instagram @johnneralcoaching.

About the Publisher

Books Change Lives: Whose life will you touch with yours?
Reach out for a personal approach to book writing and publishing.

Made in the USA
Las Vegas, NV
18 August 2021

28430917R00154